Making Pupil Data Powerful

a guide for classroom teachers

**Maggie Pringle
& Tony Cobb**

Published by Network Educational Press Ltd.
PO Box 635
Stafford
ST16 1BF

First Published 1999
© Maggie Pringle and Tony Cobb 1999

ISBN 1 85539 052 3

Maggie Pringle and Tony Cobb assert the moral right to be
identified as the authors of this work.

Series Editor - Tim Brighouse
Edited by Carol Etherington
Design & layout by
Neil Hawkins of Devine Design
Cover illustration by Darren Weaver
Internal illustrations by Joe Rice

Printed in Great Britain by
Redwood Books, Trowbridge, Wilts.

Foreword

A teacher's task is much more ambitious than it used to be and demands a focus on the subtleties of teaching and learning and on the emerging knowledge of school improvement.

This is what this series is about.

Teaching can be a very lonely activity. The time honoured practice of a single teacher working alone in the classroom is still the norm; yet to operate alone is, in the end, to become isolated and impoverished. This series addresses two issues – the need to focus on practical and useful ideas connected with teaching and learning and the wish thereby to provide some sort of an antidote to the loneliness of the long distance teacher who is daily berated by an anxious society.

Teachers flourish best when, in key stage teams or departments (or more rarely whole schools), their talk is predominantly about teaching and learning and where, unconnected with appraisal, they are privileged to observe each other teach; to plan and review their work together; and to practise the habit of learning from each other new teaching techniques. But how does this state of affairs arise? Is it to do with the way staffrooms are physically organised so that the walls bear testimony to interesting articles and in the corner there is a dedicated computer tuned to 'conferences' about SEN, school improvement, the teaching of English etc., and whether, in consequence, the teacher leaning over the shoulder of the enthusiastic IT colleague sees the promise of interesting practice elsewhere? Has the primary school cracked it when it organises successive staff meetings in different classrooms and invites the 'host' teacher to start the meeting with a 15 minute exposition of their classroom organisation and management? Or is it the same staff sharing, on a rota basis, a slot on successive staff meeting agenda when each in turn reviews a new book they have used with their class? And what of the whole school which now uses 'active' and 'passive' concerts of carefully chosen music as part of their accelerated learning techniques?

It is of course well understood that excellent teachers feel threatened when first they are observed. Hence the epidemic of trauma associated with OFSTED. The constant observation of the teacher in training seems like that of the learner driver. Once you have passed your test and can drive unaccompanied, you do. You often make lots of mistakes and sometimes get into bad habits. Woe betide, however, the back seat driver who tells you so. In the same way, the new teacher quickly loses the habit of observing others and being observed. So how do we get a confident, mutual observation debate going? One school I know found a simple and therefore brilliant solution. The Head of the History Department asked that a young colleague plan lessons for her – the Head of Department – to teach. This lesson she then taught, and was observed by the young colleague. There was subsequent discussion, in which the young teacher asked,

> *"Why did you divert the question and answer session I had planned?"*

and was answered by,

> *"Because I could see that I needed to arrest the attention of the group by the window with some 'hands-on' role play, etc."*

This lasted an hour and led to a once-a-term repeat discussion which, in the end, was adopted by the whole school. The whole school subsequently changed the pattern of its meetings to consolidate extended debate about teaching and learning. The two teachers claimed that, because one planned and the other taught, both were implicated but neither alone was responsible or felt 'got at'.

So there are practices which are both practical and more likely to make teaching a rewarding and successful activity. They can, as it were, increase the likelihood of a teacher surprising the pupils into understanding or doing something they did not think they could do rather than simply entertaining them or worse still occupying them. There are ways of helping teachers judge the best method of getting pupil expectation just ahead of self-esteem.

This series focuses on straightforward interventions which individual schools and teachers use to make life more rewarding for themselves and those they teach. Teachers deserve nothing less, for they are the architects of tomorrow's society, and society's ambition for what they achieve increases as each year passes.

Professor Tim Brighouse

Contents

Introduction   7

Chapter 1   Predicting Performance   9

Chapter 2   Setting Targets   31

Chapter 3   Using the Data   47

Chapter 4   Continuity and Progression   63

Chapter 5   Creating a Classroom Climate for Learning   79

Appendix   Sources of Further Information   99

Introduction

When schools were first required to set targets, many people believed that it would be impossible to predict pupils' performance with any degree of accuracy. It was felt to be a process in which a lot of guesswork would be involved. Different cohorts of pupils perform in different ways; some year groups and classes 'gel' better than others. All that we would be able to do would be to pluck figures out of the air: it would be just crystal ball gazing!

Schools are data-rich environments, but often the data remains the responsibility of one or two key senior staff or is filed away without impacting on teaching and learning in the school. As busy classroom and subject teachers, you may feel that you have no direct access to the data or that your workload prevents you from having time to explore effective ways of using the data that is collected.

We recognise the pressures on classroom teachers and aim to help you to get the best from your pupils. We explain how to interpret national initiatives on data-analysis, benchmarking and target-setting and ensure that these have value in the classroom. We propose ways of using pupil performance data to enhance teaching and learning.

This book offers practical support to classroom teachers in primary, middle and secondary schools. Using straightforward, manageable techniques for recording data on pupil performance, we aim to help busy teachers to interpret the information and to use it to support improved teaching and learning.

We give advice on how you can:

- analyse class and individual pupil performance and learning behaviours;
- measure progress in attainment and pupils' motivation to learn;
- predict future pupil attainment;
- set targets for improved attainment in class and for personal development;
- ensure continuity and progression in learning;
- understand and use nationally produced data for schools.

We have included case-study evidence from a range of types of school to illustrate how you can be selective in choosing information that makes the greatest impact on teaching and learning. Examples of analysis show how you can answer the following questions at whole-school, departmental, year-group, class and individual pupil level:

- How well are we doing?
- How well might we be doing?
- What do we need to do to improve?

Most people perform better when their current achievement is acknowledged and they are challenged positively and supportively to exceed their current level of attainment. We believe that pupils and their parents should be involved in understanding what pupil data is collected, what it means and how it can be used to improve performance; thus strengthening the home-school partnership, a current priority for many schools.

We hope that working through this book will help you to take the mystique out of target-setting, and to make sure that your pupil performance data becomes powerful rather than the object of the crystal-ball gazing technique.

Maggie Pringle and Tony Cobb

Chapter 1

PREDICTING PERFORMANCE

'Begin with the end in mind.'

S. Covey: Seven habits of highly effective people

> **This chapter looks at the use of data to predict a pupil's future performance. It offers help with:**
>
> ☞ **identifying your values and aspirations for your pupils, and relating these to the departmental, school, LEA and national expectations;**
>
> ☞ **shaping these into practical and challenging targets for predicted improvement;**
>
> ☞ **sources of easily accessible advice, support and information.**

Teacher aspirations

Predicting future pupil performance is not an exact science. However, we do have to do better than the quite sweeping claims of many school mission statements aiming to 'achieve a child's potential', whatever that may be!

Accurate prediction involves taking a risk, a recognised quality in good leadership and management. Your skill in collecting, analysing and acting on good data and information will be fully used. Initially, there may be more errors than you would like. Your critics will use the irritatingly exact science of hindsight! As elsewhere in teaching, experience will soon begin to have an increasing influence on 'getting it right'. Year by year, your databank will become more sophisticated, including the recorded, measurable achievement of your pupils in your classroom or subject area, influencing the way you and your team do things in the future.

No doubt you had plans for your last summer holiday - a kind of prediction of what you hoped to achieve. The camping holiday was good, but if only you had packed ... chosen to go to ... well, next year, you'll make quite sure ... . The same thought processes apply to all daily activities such as DIY, keeping fit or running a family. We all need to feel that we are looking forward, albeit a little uncertainly - trying to maximise an opportunity, and minimise risk of disappointment. It is no different in the classroom.

Your values and expectations

It is early September. Largely well intentioned and groomed new pupils sit waiting in almost unnatural attentiveness in this country's schools. You are weighing your class up. And just as certainly, they are weighing you up. What do you expect them to do better in your classroom in twelve months time - or in five years time? Stop now and fill in the diagram overleaf, however roughly.

Chapter contents

■ Teacher aspirations

■ Recognising prior attainment

■ National and local data

■ Constructing a class baseline

■ Predicting performance

Aspirations

In 12 months time, I intend that this class should:

● understand and use the following knowledge and skills from my subject teaching:

....

....

....

....

....

● show good learning behaviours such as   ....

....

....

....

● exhibit good social behaviours such as   ....

....

....

....

Using National Curriculum Teacher Assessment

In .... (subject), ... (number of) pupils in this class should be working at

Level .... by the end of the year.

I hope that the whole class achieves at least .... (description of levels attained and/or

skills and content covered) .... by the end of the year.

Are you satisfied with the targets you have set?
- Are your pupils going to feel 'challenged' by your expectations?
- Have you frightened yourself or have you been cautious?
- Are you going to tell your pupils what you expect?
- How are you going to do this, and when?

More importantly, what was the basis for your expectations? Were your expectations influenced by:
- your own values and experiences of effective learning and social behaviours?
- a knowledge of what similar pupils have achieved previously?
- your support for the agreed departmental and school objectives and targets?
- an awareness of LEA and/or national benchmark measures of pupil potential in your subject?
- careful consideration of the pupils' prior attainment, and the strengths which they have brought with them?

Were the influences on your judgement equal in significance or did they become significantly weaker as you moved down the list? In thinking about predicting future pupil achievement, prior attainment is the most important influence on that prediction.

Recognising prior attainment

'Prior attainment allows us to account for over 50 per cent of the variability between different pupils' examination results.'

Professor David Jesson: *The Numbers Game*

Treading familiar ground

Here is a familiar way of planning for the future:
A Where are the pupils now?
B Where do we want them to be, in six months ... 1 year ... 3 years?
C How do we get them from A to B?

Data and the planning process

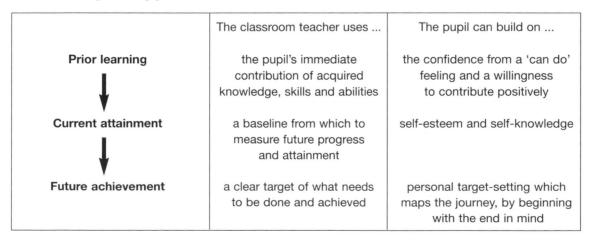

	The classroom teacher uses ...	The pupil can build on ...
Prior learning	the pupil's immediate contribution of acquired knowledge, skills and abilities	the confidence from a 'can do' feeling and a willingness to contribute positively
Current attainment	a baseline from which to measure future progress and attainment	self-esteem and self-knowledge
Future achievement	a clear target of what needs to be done and achieved	personal target-setting which maps the journey, by beginning with the end in mind

Prior learning and current attainment combine in what is known as prior attainment. This provides the baseline from which you can measure future progress and improvement.

Often in middle and secondary schools, an understandable culture develops which offers new entrants 'a fresh start in a new school'. An emphasis is put on new opportunities within the curriculum and the general life of school, as a way of motivating pupils who in many cases are already excited and productively anxious about what is ahead. We also have to recognise a degree of traditional staffroom scepticism about the information on standards of achievement passed on by the feeder school.

Issues surrounding continuity and progression are dealt with in Chapter 4, but there are evident dangers in not recognising the prior achievements of our new pupils. They have such a bearing on later results. As teachers, we have also been known to be very frustrated and feel under-valued when it is assumed that, like Manuel from Fawlty Towers, 'We know nothing'. Prior attainment - what a pupil knows now - must be the starting point for predicting future improvement.

In my school, what do I know about any new intake pupil?

Schools have always kept a variety of pupil assessment. Its use has become much more significant since the introduction of the National Curriculum and the requirement to publish results. The commonly-used school data on new pupils comes from four principal sources:

- the individual feeder school's records;
- assessment on entry by the receiving school, including Year 1 baseline assessment;
- the LEA's assessment data advisory service;
- the national publication of summarised results and comment.

When a pupil enters your classroom for the first time, you also begin to build a simple database of information. The tricky bit is in deciding what kinds of data are most useful to you. What is the baseline against which you can measure any future improvement? Two proposals appear later in the chapter.

National and local data

Principle sources of data

If you are to predict future pupil attainment, selective data gathering needs to be done from the following four sources of local and national data. The simple table below mirrors the advice to headteachers and governors in the DfEE's *From targets to action*. Here it is amended for your use in the classroom:

Feeder schools	Assessment on entry
LEA information	National information

Feeder schools

In recent years, schools have made strenuous efforts to improve links with each other. Feeder schools provide the best data on an individual pupil's current performance. It is still probably true that great variety exists in two areas of information giving:

- in the varied range of evidence on performance, skills, attitude and interests available to each pupil's new school;

- in the extent to which this information is made available generally, or in part, to the school's classroom teachers.

Check what information is available now to you or the curriculum area in which you work and complete the table overleaf. It may be helpful to talk through your understanding with a senior colleague.

Having completed it, there are now a number of related questions.

- How is this information going to improve teaching and learning in my classroom?
- Do I need to know all the information which is available? How does it help learning in my subject(s)?
- Is some information better not known? We are all grateful sometimes for a fresh start. Would your attitude to some pupils be different if you knew less about them initially?

What is clear is that national education policy now demands that all teachers give attention to the achievement of measurable results in National Curriculum subjects - in reality, to the achievement of measurable improvement. The current target-setting initiative confirms this.

Assessment on entry

Your school or subject area may use some form of screening test when pupils arrive in the school. Not every school does this. If it is true of your school, explore the reasons why specific kinds of information are being collected. How is this information used? Generally, screening for additional information is intended to provide:

- a baseline and tested predictions of future performance by individual pupils;

- a means of grouping pupils in classes in ways determined by the school.

Two more commonly used forms of pupil screening are:

- The family of information systems offered by the Curriculum, Evaluation and Management Centre at the University of Durham. The systems monitor the progress made by pupils (the value-added), their self-esteem and the quality of life within the school. You may recognise them by the following acronyms:

  PIPS: Performance indicators in primary schools
  MIDYIS: Middle years information system
  YELLIS: Year 11 information system
  ALIS: Advanced Level information system

Information about new pupils

	EXAMPLES OF INFORMATION	NOTE YOUR SCHOOL'S INFORMATION	SOURCE OF INFORMATION
All schools should receive ...	Test and Teacher Assessment results for the three core subjects, English, mathematics and science		
	records of standardised tests used by individual feeder schools		
Many schools may receive ...	indications of special skills such as IT, music, sport		
	pointers to current personal interests, e.g. recreational or hobby pursuits		
	comments on attendance, behaviour, inter-personal skills		
Some schools will want to screen new pupils for ...	information gleaned from tests such as Cognitive Ability Tests		
	additional subject specific knowledge, skills and abilities		

© Network Educational Press

- NFER Cognitive Ability Tests (CATs) are used by many secondary schools, usually in Years 7 and 9. Three tests (verbal, quantitative, non-verbal) are used for screening all pupils, and the data is regarded as one good indicator of future attainment. The data also prompts a look at pupils who may be under achieving, or indeed significantly exceeding expectations.

Other forms of nationally recognised standardised tests, servicing agencies and subject-based assessments are also used.

LEA information

The LEA's assessment data advisory service could be a very useful source of information for you. Given your own workload, it is worth checking what the LEA is able to provide in your subject area. Many LEAs have produced their own booklets of good advice. The cliché 'reinventing the wheel' has been used so often that it is no wonder that educational bandwagons have a momentum which exhausts us all! Use others' helpful advice.

The role of the LEA is significant in monitoring, reviewing and evaluating the work of the schools in its area. The School Standards and Framework Act 1998 details this. There are national targets for achievement. Each LEA has been given an indicative target of measurable achievement by the end of Key Stages 2 and 4. Your headteacher, governors, senior staff and a variety of community interests are aware of these expectations.

National Targets KS2
By 2002:

- 80% of 11 year olds will have reached Level 4 in English
- 75% of 11 year olds will have reached Level 4 in mathematics

National Targets KS4
By 2002:

- 50% of 16 year olds will obtain 5+ A*-C Grades at GCSE
- 90% of 16 year olds will obtain 1+ A*-G Grades at GCSE

Schools are also required to set targets for the average points score per pupil at GCSE.

Overleaf, you can see the practical implications at Key Stage 2.

Expectations of LEAs: Percentage of Level 4 English at Key Stage 2

	1996 percentage	By 2002
Durham	57%	81%
Newcastle upon Tyne	49%	80%
Gateshead	57%	85%
Northumberland	58%	83%
Sunderland	55%	85%

National data collection is now adding information about the general performance of pupils in core subjects at the end of each key stage.

It is possible to see how your class compares with the national performance generally, and how your class compares with pupils from similar schools.

Percentage of pupils at each level in English tests at Key stage 2

School results compared with national figures (boys and girls combined)

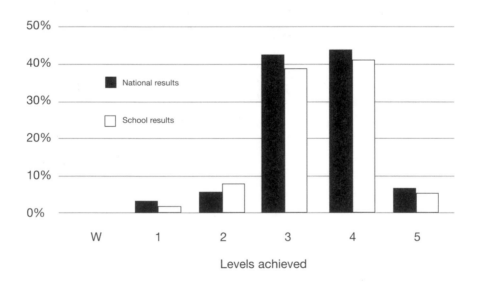

Levels achieved

National information

You will need to look at national information which your school is sent annually. Be selective, and see this data mainly as a guide about what it is possible to achieve with similar pupils. It sets your school-based data into a wider context, and will be used as one factor in assessing how your classes are performing within the overall performance of your school.

You need to be aware of two nationally advocated assessment tools:

- Benchmarking — ask to look at the school's PANDA, which is discussed opposite.
- Chances graphs — ask to look at the school's Autumn Package.

Benchmarking

'Benchmarking is the term given to the process of measuring standards of actual performance against those achieved by others (schools) with broadly similar characteristics, identifying best practice. ... Benchmarking shows the standards achieved by the best members of the group (the best 25% of schools nationally) and presents sound contextual information to assist schools in setting their own targets.'

QCA 1997: Consultation Paper

Once again, the core subjects are the focus for benchmarking but teachers of other National Curriculum subjects should find the information useful in understanding aspects of their pupils' general abilities. Currently, schools are grouped for benchmarking purposes on measures of:

- the percentage of pupils entitled to free school meals;

- the extent of pupil selection on the basis of ability (secondary);

- the percentage of pupils with English as an additional language (primary).

The benchmarking data for your school is in your PANDA, produced by OFSTED. When schools first received their PANDAs, early in 1998, OFSTED advised that the information was being sent 'to enable you (schools) to see how your school compares with others and to help you in the development of plans to raise standards ... to aid self-evaluation, as a starting point for self improvement'.

The contents of the PANDA are set out in the adjacent panel. It is interesting whole-school information. Be aware of its contents, used by many to measure a school's effectiveness. However, you may feel that you need a more selective look, concentrating upon your own class performances, or that of your subject area, and comparing this with comparable national results.

Performance and assessment (PANDA)

A PANDA contains:

- basic characteristics of the school:
- number on roll
- % of pupils with English as an additional language
- % of pupils entitled to free school meals
- number of pupils with special educational needs and statements

- a description of school context, including:
- % of adults in higher education
- % of pupils in higher class social households
- % of minority ethnic children
- % of children in overcrowded households
- attendance figures

- analysis of school performance in core subjects

- a wider range of subject performance indicators at Key Stage 4.

At Key Stages 1, 2 and 3, a typical benchmarking table looks like this, with only slight variations in the information given at each key stage:

Example of benchmark reporting in PANDA: KS1/2/3

Non-selective schools with up to 5% FSM

Percentile	95th	Upper Quartile		60th		40th		Lower Quartile		5th	Interpretation
Percentage pupils reaching Level 5 or above											
English (TA)	94	85	**83**	80		76		71		60	B
English (tests)	95	87		84		78	**75**	73		62	D
Mathematics (TA)	95	85		82		77	**75**	74		66	D
Mathematics (tests)	90	81		78		74		71	**69**	65	E
Science (TA)	93	86		83	**81**	78		74		66	C
Science(tests)	91	82		78		74		70	**64**	61	E
Percentage pupils reaching Level 6 or above											
English (TA)	67	51		46		39	**38**	33		22	D
English (tests)	75	59		52	**45**	44		38		24	C
Mathematics (TA)	76	60		54		49		45	**45**	32	E
Mathematics (tests)	73	59		54		50	**49**	46		38	D
Science (TA)	69	55		50	**47**	42		38		24	C
Science(tests)	66	51		45		41	**39**	36		25	D

The interpretation codes are as follows:

A*: pupils' results were **very high** in comparison with other schools with pupils from similar backgrounds.

A: pupils' results were **well above** average in comparison with other schools with pupils from similar backgrounds.

B: pupils' results were **above average** in comparison with schools with pupils from similar backgrounds.

C: pupils' results were **broadly average** in comparison with schools with pupils from similar backgrounds.

D: pupils' results were **below average** in comparison with schools with pupils from similar backgrounds.

E: pupils' results were **well below** average in comparison with schools with pupils from similar backgrounds.

E*: pupils' results were **very low** in comparison with schools with pupils from similar backgrounds.

What can we learn from the PANDA benchmarking table?

Ask yourself what questions are prompted by the above table of results. If it was recording your school's attainment, what would you want to know more about? Beware of drawing immediate conclusions from such a table until you have explored the situations which produced each set of data. Each school's analysis should then influence its next actions.

Try these prompts:

- What interpretation do you put on the difference between the percentages for Teacher Assessment and those for the Tests, particularly for English and Science? Is the school's assessment sufficiently challenging?

- Is the work which is assessed being given greater teaching priority than that which is tested?

● What can be learned from the higher level attainments? Are teacher expectations too low, or too high?

Next, you can begin to test your initial thoughts by investigating further and looking at other evidence.

Later in the chapter, you will see that the same benchmarking table has become more sophisticated. Instead of using the school's percentage of pupils with free meals entitlement, the benchmarking uses prior attainment as the basis for grouping schools.

Data of this kind is a very useful guide, prompting questions when reviewing and evaluating teaching and learning. The data adds to our understanding of how pupils are currently performing. Like a thermometer, it will provide a layperson with a measure of the subject's health. An informed professional then adds other data, experience and skill to judge whether the patient is very fit, getting better, or in fact has a cold, flu or pneumonia. As the classroom teacher, you are the professional closest to the 'patient' and will be expected increasingly to interpret and act upon data information.

Key Stage 4 information is shown in the PANDA in this way:

Comparison of School's performance with National benchmarks, GCSE/GNVQ results

Non-selective schools with up to 5% FSM

Percentile	95th	Upper Quartile	60th	40th		Lower Quartile		5th	Interpretation
5+GCSE A*-C or GNVQ equivalent	82	69	66	61		57	**53**	46	**E**
5+GCSE A*-G or GNVQ equivalent	100	98	97	96	**94**	94		91	**D**
1+GCSE A*-G or GNVQ equivalent	100	99	99	98		97	**96**	95	**E**
Average total GCSE/GNVQ point score per pupil	55	47	46	43	**43**	42		38	**D**

The interpretation codes are as follows:

A*: pupils' results were **very high** in comparison with other schools with pupils from similar backgrounds.

A: pupils' results were **well above average** in comparison with other schools with pupils from similar backgrounds.

B: pupils' results were **above average** in comparison with schools with pupils from similar backgrounds.

C: pupils' results were **broadly average** in comparison with schools with pupils from similar backgrounds.

D: pupils' results were **below average** in comparison with schools with pupils from similar backgrounds.

E: pupils' results were **well below average** in comparison with schools with pupils from similar backgrounds.

E*: pupils' results were **very low** in comparison with schools with pupils from similar backgrounds.

It is not surprising that national data on pupil performance has gained a greater significance:

- The National Curriculum has become established, with its four compulsory stages for testing and teacher assessment.
- The results of these formal assessments are being published, and commentators may spice the information by producing 'league tables'.
- The parent or guardian of every child has a nationally comparable result that measures their child's performance at each of the four stages.

Constructing a class baseline

Establish a National Curriculum baseline for your new pupils

The school's assessment co-ordinator should be building a table of data, showing how your school's new intake performs at each key stage. It should be possible to extrapolate the data for your class quite easily.

This chapter has drawn attention to the rapid growth in the quantity and quality of data sent to schools annually. In the three core subjects, it is possible to look at the profile of your class in terms of National Curriculum levels achieved, and compare your pupils' results with national attainment at any key stage. Benchmarking adds comparison with pupils from similar schools.

In order to help teachers, commercial trials have been conducted looking at ICT's contributions to recording National Curriculum levels for individual pupils, and in providing analysis of the results. A telephone call to QCA, or commercial companies serving other school data needs, would establish the latest position.

Key Stage 1

Many LEAs have developed their own patterns of baseline assessment for pupils when they first start school. Here is an example from Bedfordshire LEA, taken from its Lower Schools' booklet on target-setting.

Baseline data for pupils aged 5: Bedfordshire LEA

Pupil	*abcd* results 1996 English	Predicted Y2 - 1999 English	Y1 1997 Reading TA	Predicted Y2 - 1999 Reading	Target Y2 - 1999 Reading
A	6	3	1	2	
B	1	W	W	W	
C	7	3/4	1/2	3/4	
D	3	1	W	1	
E	5	2	1	1/2	
F	6	3	1	3	

Making Pupil Data Powerful - a guide for classroom teachers

Bedfordshire's *abcd* assessment result is designed to help schools to set Key Stage 1 targets. It is based on the QCA gradings for Level 2, with minor amendments, and is used particularly to predict performance in reading. Your own LEA may well have such a scheme, many of which record a wide range of knowledge, skills and learning behaviours. This book is simply seeking to establish the principle of using prior attainment, and, as a class teacher, you will want a simple but perceptive method of recording baseline assessment.

Key Stages 2, 3 and 4

Establishing a baseline becomes easier to do if you teach one of the three core subjects. However, the patterns of recording below could apply to any National Curriculum subject. The example below looks at progress through Key Stage 3.

The choice and time-span of the data is yours, subject to the agreed assessment policy and achievement targets of your department and the school.

Recording subject data at the start of Key Stage 3

Pupil Level	NC Reading PIPS score	CAT score/ subject level or other St'd test	KS2 level achieved, where known	Level predicted end of Year 7	Level predicted end of Year 8	Level predicted end of Year 9
Asif						
Bevan						
Chloe						
Diana						

Feeder school   Your school   Feeder school   Your professional judgement

Sources of data

Notes

- **NC reading level** can be a useful guide for you. Are you sure that the majority of pupils in your class can read your written resources with understanding? Any tabloid newspaper responds to this information in order to stay in business.

- **CAT/PIPS and other standardised forms of assessment**, used on or just after entry to the school, were discussed earlier in this chapter (see pages 13-15). All nationally required results refer to NC levels but it is very useful to develop a complementary source of standardised data which helps us to a better judgement of a pupil's abilities.

- **NC level for KS2, in your subject** - in the core subjects, this will be essential information for you. It is already known by the pupil and parent. In non-core subjects, you may not have this information for a variety of reasons, particularly if you are only now making a start in a subject such as modern languages.

- **Your own professional judgement** is at the heart of any prediction about future performance, based upon:
  - the current assessment, if available;
  - your experience with similar pupils over the years;
  - your interpretation of the 'chances' of success, using the kind of model described later in this chapter.

As we said at the beginning of the book, this is not an exact science. The collected data will help to shape and influence your thinking and planning - but it should never prescribe what happens to pupils in your charge. It is important, too, that you also:

- ask the pupils what they think they can achieve in your subject. Many of the answers may hearten, alarm or depress you - or they may indeed confirm a shared view. (More of this in Chapter 2.)

- inform, and if possible, harness the positive interest of parents in supporting their children, where data can be shown to point to specific learning needs.

Predicting performance

The National Curriculum levels are very broad. Generally it is assumed that:

- an average pupil aged 7 will achieve National Curriculum Level 2;

- an average pupil aged 11 will achieve National Curriculum Level 4;

- an average pupil aged 14 will achieve National Curriculum Level 5/6.

We know that pupils progress at different rates. Many schools are now recording how their pupils are performing over two key stages in order to measure a number of factors, including pupil progress, the school's 'value added', and to predict future performance. Ashcombe School in Surrey included the following guidance in information for parents:

Information for parents: Ashcombe School, Surrey

Key Stage 3 GCSE predictions	
Average KS3 Level	**Range of individual predictions of grade**
Average Level 3	Grades F & E
Average Level 4	Mainly grades F, E & D - some Cs
Average Level 5	Mainly grades D & C - some Es and Bs
Average Level 6	Mainly grades C & B - some Ds and As
Average Level 7	Mainly grades B & A - some Cs and A*s
Average Level 8	Mainly grades A and A* - some Bs

Parrs Wood High School in Manchester used a diagram like the one opposite to illustrate likely outcomes through the two secondary key stages. Using KS2 data and reading scores, the school has constructed six pupil descriptor bands and predicted likely outcomes at the end of KS3 and GCSE for each band (see opposite).

Predicting performance throughout KS3 and 4 : Parrs Wood High School, Manchester

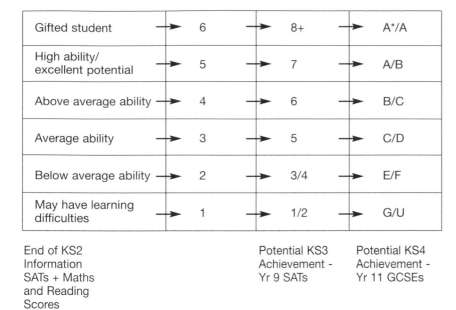

Gifted student	→ 6	→ 8+	→ A*/A
High ability/ excellent potential	→ 5	→ 7	→ A/B
Above average ability	→ 4	→ 6	→ B/C
Average ability	→ 3	→ 5	→ C/D
Below average ability	→ 2	→ 3/4	→ E/F
May have learning difficulties	→ 1	→ 1/2	→ G/U

End of KS2
Information
SATs + Maths
and Reading
Scores

Potential KS3
Achievement –
Yr 9 SATs

Potential KS4
Achievement –
Yr 11 GCSEs

With larger numbers of pupils, it is possible to give this kind of guidance, based on the school's own recorded evidence. However, you may find that you need to refine the data evidence, particularly if it is to be used to identify and improve strengths and weaknesses in individual pupils' learning.

Begin to refine your data

Teacher assessment becomes a very important tool in accurately assessing a pupil's progress. Many schools and LEAs are looking at ways of refining achievement within the levels, using the evidence from regular teacher assessment. The following frequently used example illustrates the point, and the coding applies within any National Curriculum level:

> **Refining within National Curriculum levels**
> Based on Teacher Assessment information, grade pupils a, b or c within each level.
>
> a   Only just crossed the threshold of this level;
>
> b   Working securely at this level;
>
> c   Beginning to work at the next level.
>
> Example: A pupil recorded as Level 3c would be described as beginning to work at Level 4.

At Key Stages 1 and 2, it is advisable to check the teacher assessments refined in this way against other standardised indicators of attainment, such as validated reading and numeracy tests. Other popular forms of complementary assessment were discussed earlier in this chapter (see pages 13-15).

Discussion with other colleagues in order to agree the sub-divisions within levels of achievement has to be beneficial. Given the breadth of the levels, and the difficulty we all have in confidently assessing levels of achievement in many subjects, such discussion helps to promote:

- consistency and moderation in assessment;
- the sharing of assessment experience and techniques;
- a better appreciation of what is being assessed;
- a picture of how the assessments can be used most effectively to improve pupil performance;
- the general sharing of good practice in teaching and learning.

What does 'working securely at this level' mean in practice? What kinds of work and activity best illustrate this?

What precisely do my colleagues expect in terms of future attainment and measured progress from my class?

Predicting performance for your class at the end of any key stage
Example: by the end of Key Stage 2

Stage 1

Your class is currently at the end of Year 4. Using the abc coding within levels, their current attainment is as follows:

Coding at end of KS1	Pupils' names	Coding at Year 4	Pupils' names
1b	Tracy, Diana	2b	Tracy, Imran
1c	Jon, Lee, Imran	2c	Morgan, Diana, Jon
2a	Paula, Peter, Saeed	3a	Paula, Peter, Lee
2b	Fatima, Dale, Asif, Chloe	3b	Kerry, Fatima, Dale, Saeed
2c	Zara, George	3c	George, Asif, Chloe
		4a	Zara

When recording the range of National Curriculum Levels achieved for the first time, you may well be using a mix of experience and a range of QCA Y4 and other standardised material to assess attainment. The shaded line represents the attainment of approximately 60% of your pupils - a guiding 'norm' against which subsequent years can be compared and improved. Other forms of coding within NC levels can be decided to suit your school if you wish. However, abc is in fairly common use and allows for easy comparison.

Stage 2

An assessment of the predicted KS2 attainment of individual pupils is the next essential stage in the process. Chapter 2 focuses on this in full. You will see that a range of factors will influence the progress of individual children, and groups of pupils. Your aggregated predictions of individual pupils (shaded column) will guide your prediction for the class as a whole.

Name of pupil	End of KS1	Year 4	Predicted at end of KS2	Learning targets and support (see Chapter 2)
Asif	2b	3c	4c	
Chloe	2b	3c	3c	
Dale	2b	3c	4a	
Douglas	1b	2b	3a	
Fatima	2b	3b	4b	

Stage 3

Now agree with the headteacher or subject co-ordinator a realistic set of targets for your pupils and also a class target. Chapter 2 continues from this point:

Target = Prediction + Challenge

Chances graphs

The chances of winning the national lottery are said to be 14 million to 1. Apparently, there is a higher chance of being struck by lightning. What are the more realistic chances of 60% of your class getting Level 4 at age 11, or Level 5/6 at age 14?

The DfEE/OFSTED/QCA Autumn Package, sent to every school, invites you to look at your pupils' future chances of achieving expectations or exceeding them, based on their measured prior attainment. The contents include:

● the 1998 national summary of results;

● tables of benchmark information to enable comparisons between similar schools;

● value-added information (not at KS1) including chances graphs;

● optional activities designed to help teachers using comparative data for the first time.

Section 1c in the package deals with chances graphs for all key stages.

1998 was an important year for data recording for National Curriculum Tests and Teacher Assessment.

Secondary schools

For the first time, nationally collated data shows how the same cohort of pupils achieved in the core subjects at two different key stages. All secondary school pupils were tested and assessed for the first time in 1995, and the three-year interval to 1998 allows 1995 KS2 results to be compared with 1998 KS3 results for the same pupils. It is now possible to look at an individual pupil's attainment at Key Stage 2 and predict the chances of achieving at a range of appropriate levels in three years time, based on existing proven evidence.

Primary Schools

Section 1c has the same chances graphs, and the same opportunity to see nationally how a pupil with a specific attainment level at KS1 might be expected to perform four years later at KS2. For the purist, the Summer 1999 national results will provide the first record of how all the country's children progressed between the 1995 KS1 tests and teacher assessment, over the four-year gap to KS2 in 1999.

Prior attainment will increasingly determine the grouping of schools for benchmarking purposes, replacing current criteria such as percentage of pupils with free-meal entitlement or English as an additional language.

Using prior attainment, the actual results achieved by all pupils nationally at Key Stage 2 are shown for groups of pupils who shared the same average level of attainment at Key Stage 1.

The average range for each grouping of pupils at the previous key stage is decided by the average of the levels achieved in the core subjects. (The same practice is followed at Key Stages 3 and 4, with examples in the appropriate Autumn Package.)

Five examples are given, each illustrating a different level of prior attainment at KS1, and the later attainment at KS2. Two are shown here.

1.33 <=Key Stage 1 Average Test/Task Level <= 1.75

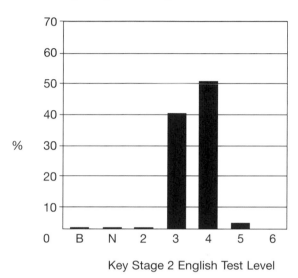

Key Stage 2 English Test Level

2.33 <= Key Stage 1 Average Test/Task Level <= 2.67

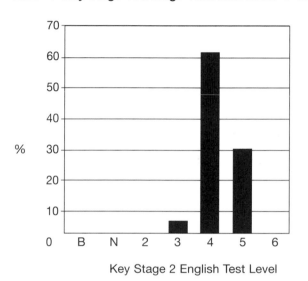

Key Stage 2 English Test Level

Benchmarking tables

Using prior attainment, these tables show the percentage of pupils attaining the standard range of GCSE targets at Key Stage 4 in 1998, from schools whose pupils shared the same average level of attainment in core subjects at Key Stage 3 in 1996. The Autumn Package currently shows six tables, each illustrating a different average attainment in core subjects at KS3 and the subsequent attainment at KS4 for each group. One example is shown here.

All schools that achieved a Key Stage 3 average level of more than 4.5 and up to 5.0 in 1996

Percentage of pupils	95%	UQ	60%	Median	40%	LQ	5%
English GCSE A* - C	65	55	50	48	45	42	32
Maths GCSE A* - C	55	46	41	39	36	33	24
Science GCSE A* - C	61	50	45	42	40	35	23
5+ GCSE/GNVQs A* - C	58	49	45	42	40	36	27
5+ GCSE/GNVQs A* - G	98	95	93	92	91	88	81
1+ GCSE/GNVQs A*-G	100	98	97	96	95	94	90

Percentage of schools achieving:

	95%	UQ	60%	Median	40%	LQ	5%
GCSE/GNVQ PS 6	43	39	37	36	35	33	29

(number of schools: 1,132)

Ashcombe School in Surrey looked at GCSE points scores and the probability of their better than average pupil-intake achieving scores of between 65 and 76 points at GCSE. They then suggested crude betting chances. They drew similarities with the number of points required by Manchester United to win the Premiership, or to share prices achieving a particular price in three months time. For their own school they produced the following table:

score	probability of achieving it	betting chances (approx.)
65	99%	100 to 1 on
67	95%	20 to 1 on
69	75%	3 to 1 on
72	50%	evens
74	25%	3 to 1
76	5%	20 to 1

Try the next example using your class or subject data.

Using existing data to predict future achievement

Your markbook can easily build up a database. Your subject area can record what happens in your school to the same pupils, whose attainment and progress are measured at the end of at least two consecutive key stages. A class and/or subject chances graph is constructed, reflecting what actually happens to pupils in your school. That too can be compared with the national results in the Autumn Package.

Using the evidence of your recorded results, you should be able to predict the results:

● If a pupil comes to you with Level 2 at the end of KS1, then the chances of achieving Level 5 at the end of KS2 are ....

● If a pupil comes with levels between 4 and 5 at the end of KS2, then the chances of achieving Level 5 in your subject area are ....

The following two chapters develop aspects of predicting and achieving future improved performance.   We have to move from:

● **retrospective analysis** - only looking at the end results and applying analyses of these to future year groups
to

● **prospective analysis** - giving greater recognition to prior attainment, and the evidence of what similar pupils can attain, to predict what our class or subject area might achieve in three or four years time. This is more exciting.

You should now be ready to look at current performance - pupils' progress with you - and to more formalised target-setting.

Action points

1. Set out your aspirations for the measurable improvement in knowledge, skills and behaviour of your class over the next 12 or 24 months.

2. Make a list of all the available attainment information known to you on your new class.

3. Decide how you are going to fill any gaps in your information from the four sources listed on pages 12 - 20.

4. Save time and gain useful advice by finding out if data analysis is already being tackled by:
   - a colleague in school;
   - a service within the Local Education Authority or other agency.

5. Read your school's PANDA, particularly the benchmarking tables. What do you learn about the potential attainment of your class?

6. Identify the particular forms of data which will provide an attainment baseline for your class.

7. Become familiar with abc or other forms of differentiation used within National Curriculum levels.

8. Read your school's copy of the Autumn Package, particularly Section 1c on valued-added and chances graphs. Estimate the chances of your class achieving a range of levels by the end of this key stage.

Chapter 2

SETTING TARGETS

'If I always do what I always did, I'll always get what I always got.'

A pupil

> **This chapter looks at setting targets with pupils. It offers help with:**
>
> ☞ **setting measurable outcome targets with pupils;**
>
> ☞ **differentiating between predicted grades and target grades;**
>
> ☞ **identifying process targets that help pupils to meet their targets;**
>
> ☞ **embedding your own practice within a school-wide system of setting targets with pupils.**

Setting pupils challenging targets

In the last chapter, we looked at how you can now predict pupils' potential performance by taking into account:

- a pupil's prior attainment;
- your experience of what similar pupils have achieved in your class/subject;
- your knowledge of what LEA/national data tells you about the progress of similar pupils.

As we have mentioned before, this is not an exact science - and never will be. For a start, there is - and always will be - a wide range of outcomes from similar levels of prior attainment, as the chances graphs demonstrate. Let's consider the chances (in NC level terms) in the Key Stage 3 test in Maths of a pupil with a Key Stage 2 average Test/Task Level 4:

Chapter contents

■ Setting pupils challenging targets

■ Helping pupils to achieve targets

■ Systems for setting targets

■ Setting school and class targets

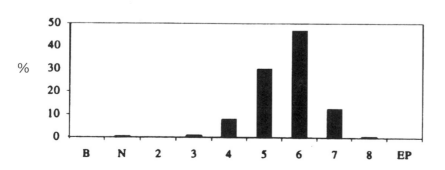

The Autumn Package, 1998, Key Stage 3

We cannot assume that Level 6 is a certainty; Level 5 is a distinct possibility, Levels 4 and 7 are clearly possible, even if 8 and 3 are a distant dream/nightmare!

What factors would lead you to predict a particular outcome from this range for a particular pupil? These might include:

- the pupil's attitude;
- the progress of similar pupils in your class;
- any other factors particular to your knowledge of that pupil.

One that needs to be added is CHALLENGE!

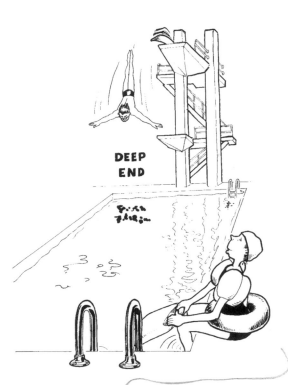

Informed educational thinking now speaks of challenging targets - realistic and achievable, but challenging. All pupils understand what this means. Who, more than our pupils, dream their dreams - of making a million, becoming an airline pilot or simply swimming two lengths of a pool when a width has yet to be managed? We should be concerned if an element of high vaulting ambition was not present in the young - or in ourselves as their teachers.

Targets are a way of adding challenge to our predictions:

Targets = Prediction + Challenge

A prediction says "This is what you are likely to achieve if you carry on as you are now."

A target says "This is what you could achieve IF . . . "

Target-setting with individual pupils is not part of the statutory scheme of target-setting. However, it is increasingly being used as a way of empowering pupils, of engaging them in the process of learning, and of defining and realising their entitlement. After all, target-setting depends on data about them and pupils like them, and our aspirations for them. It is natural that teachers are finding it motivating to involve pupils in the process.

To summarise, target-setting should result from activity in three areas:

- your consideration of the available data;
- application of 'prediction + challenge' thinking;
- stated ambition and/or self-appraisal by the pupil.

The approaches outlined next follow this process.

Target-setting at sixth-form level

Because of the data available from the ALIS (Advanced Level information system) scheme, many schools have begun pupil target-setting with sixth-form students. Students are given graphs to plot the conversion of GCSE points scores into predicted A-level performance set against national expectations. Students become aware of differing 'degrees of difficulty' between subjects, both at GCSE and A level. They have a clear indication of the likely outcome of current performance. Following this, target grades in each subject are set. Feedback from teachers, regularly expressed in terms of actual A-level grades, allows students and tutors to review progress against those targets. Tutors report that this process has had a markedly beneficial effect on the tendency for pupils to 'coast' during the first year of the A-level course. "Some students were encouraged by what the data predicted; others were downcast. Some even seemed angry, and swore that they would prove the data wrong!" Tutors were able to point out that predicted grades need not be target grades, but that targets must be realistic and achievable. Students had to consider the implications of the data. It is vital that the tutors should be given time to discuss what might happen in the target-setting dialogue with pupils and make sure that they can use the process as a positive experience for all students.

Target-setting in Year 10

Many schools have understandably wished to take advantage of the new beginning of Key Stage 4 to set targets at this time. In the past, with relatively little national progress data to call upon, schools have used their own progression rates to form the basis of discussion with pupils. Acknowledging that the mean Key Stage 3 SATs level is often the best indicator of GCSE performance, schools have set targets with pupils along the following lines:

Name	Mean KS3 SATs level	Minimum target grade
Asif	3	E
Bevan	5	C
Chloe	4	D

However, following the publication of the subject progress lines available from their LEA, schools have begun to refine their targets estimating the chances of converting, for example, a mean SAT of 4.7 in Geography into a D, C or E.

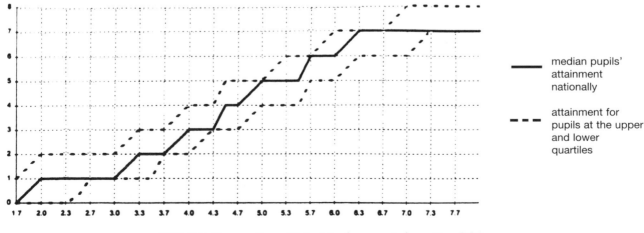

1998 LEA Compendium of School Performance Information, QCA

Increasingly, departments are customising the school system of predicting outcomes and setting targets. The example below shows how a single-line pupil profile can combine prior attainment, target grade and teacher feedback to track pupils' current performance against target grades in a particular subject.

Tracking pupils in history

Name	KS3 Teacher Assessment/ Test			Hist level	Predicted grade range	Target grade	Year 10 Dec. Assessment	Year 10 July Assessment	Revised target grade	Year 11 Jan Assessment	Year 11 Outcome	Further predictions/ targets
	Eng.	Maths	Science									
Lee	3/4	4/4	4/3	4	F/E/D	D	E/D					
Toni	5/5	5/6	5/6	5	C/B	B	B					

The experience of tracking pupils from one key stage to another has led many schools to begin to ask useful questions about the progress of pupils before that key stage. For example, teachers have asked that the school effort grade should be included so that they can begin to discuss with certain pupils the possibility of achieving a higher target grade based on the assumption that the pupils could improve their effort. Sometimes it is helpful in this context to include an earlier indicator, i.e. at Year 7, which indicates a potential well above what the pupil is currently achieving with a disappointing effort grade. One teacher reports: 'The data is far more powerful than hours of nagging on my part!'

Other teachers, recognising the significance of literacy skills to performance at GCSE, have asked for a reading age to be included. The issue for schools is to provide the maximum of useful data while keeping it manageable.

Target-setting at Key Stage 2

For some years now, primary schools have used the minimum expectation that pupils will progress 'half a National Curriculum level per year' as a way of setting measurable outcome targets with pupils and parents.

In the example opposite, Stanley County Junior School established a five-band grid based around the progress line of the average child in the age group. This grid and the expected end of Key Stage 2 levels for each band are shared with parents to allow them to see how their children are progressing in relation to their peer group and also in relation to their prior attainment.

Making Pupil Data Powerful - a guide for classroom teachers

Predicted progress in the National Curriculum for all abilities

End of year level placement and grades

Key

G   =   Grade (A, B or C according to attainment)

L   =   National Curriculum level awarded at end of year

↑   =   And above

↓   =   And below

A   =   National Curriculum level exceeded

B   =   National Curriculum level reached

C   =   Working towards National Curriculum level

□   =   Level and grade for the 'average' child in age group

	Predicted levels at end of year				
Attainment descriptors	**Y2**	**Y3**	**Y4**	**Y5**	**Y6**
Has substantially exceeded targets for age group	↑	↑	↑	↑	↑
Has exceeded targets for age groups	↑	↑	↑	↑	↑
Has reached targets for age group	LG 2B	LG 2A	LG 3B	LG 3A	LG 4B
Working towards targets (with support)	↓	↓	↓	↓	↓
Working towards targets (with substantial support)	↓	↓	↓	↓	↓

Expected end of Key Stage 2 levels for the above five groups

- Substantially exceeds targets   Level 6
- Exceeds targets   Level 5
- Reaches targets   Level 4
- Working towards (with support)   Level 3 and below
- Working towards (with substantial support)   Level 2 and below

Special note

Children will normally complete one level every two years.

Stanley County Junior School

Now try setting your own targets!

Prediction	Target = Prediction + Challenge
1. A pupil beginning Year 6 in September is assessed at Level 3a reading. At the end of Year 4, he was at Level 2c. He has made little progress since then. For the past two years, over 80% of pupils have achieved Level 4 at KS2. His parent has promised support, but you suspect the pupil of laziness. **Prediction: Level 3b at KS2**	a. Individual target at KS2: .... b. Action plan: ....
2. Your class in Year 7 comes mainly from four feeder primary schools. Their profile of science NC level is: 5 = 3 pupils 3 = 10 pupils 4 = 12 pupils 2 = 5 pupils (50% at Level 4 or above) Benchmarking data from two feeder schools puts science in the lowest quartile for last two years. Your school's KS3 results show a three-year average of 82% of pupils achieving Level 5. **Prediction: 65% gain Level 5 at KS3**	a. Class target at KS3: .... b. Action plan: ....

How did you get on? What did you make of the action plan? Perhaps you felt that you would need to know more about the pupil before you could complete it. If you thought that it was a rather different activity from setting the target, you are right. In all of the examples given, we have been discussing outcome grades, by which we mean hard, measurable outcome performance grades for our pupils. However, whether we are discussing performance at school, department or pupil level, we need to remember that there are limitations as well as strengths to performance grades. There is little doubt that outcome grades are motivating.

> "At the beginning of Year 10, we gave pupils actual grades and potential grades: pupils saw that where they are now need not be where they might have been and might be in the future. In my view, the introduction of this distinction between actual and potential (or indeed predicted and target) grades was the most successful strategy we had in raising pupils' achievement."
>
> *Deputy headteacher*

However, motivating as they are, targets do not answer the pupils' questions "But what do I have to do to achieve the targets?" In short, outcome targets need to be accompanied by process targets. Or to put it another way, the five-stage cycle of self-improvement is as relevant to the individual student as it is to the whole school.

A Five-stage cycle for School Self-improvement (QCA)

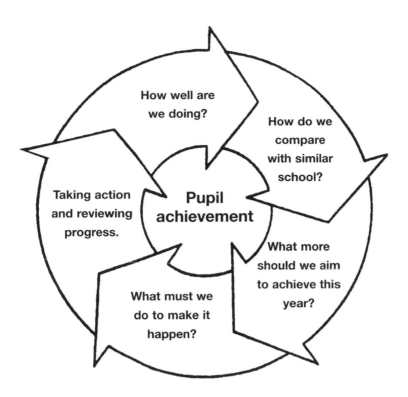

We need to move fairly swiftly from the 'what' to the 'how': "How am I going to reach the target I have been given?" Motivation is good - but not enough.

Helping pupils to achieve targets

Earlier, we defined the difference between predictions and targets:

A prediction says "This is what you are likely to achieve if you carry on as you are now."
A target says "This is what you could achieve IF... "

How could you finish that sentence?

- ... if you work harder;
- ... if you concentrate more in class;
- ... if you develop your ideas;
- ... if you read more widely;
- ... if you participate more in class;
- ... if you improve the presentation of your work.

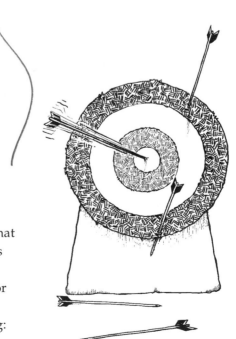

These are comments which we make all the time as teachers and which were probably made to us as pupils! But are we really sure that pupils know how to act on them? Some of these are life-long targets for some pupils! Are we sure that these targets are sufficiently SMART - specific, measurable, achievable, realistic, time-related - for pupils to use? Are we sure that they answer the observation sometimes made about the centrality of feedback to pupils' learning:

'Children rarely received the kind of feedback on their work that helped them to know what or how to improve.'

Access and Achievement in Urban Education, HMSO 1993

'Marking frequently focuses on completion and presentation, neglecting strengths and weaknesses and failing to inform pupils what they must do to improve.'

The Annual Report of HMCI of Schools, 1999

Providing the kind of feedback that strengthens the link between assessment and effective learning is not, of course, confined to target-setting. Teachers may achieve it in a variety of ways; by their marking or by informal dialogue with pupils in the classroom. Chris Dickinson, in Section Three of *Effective Learning Activities* gives further examples. However, the process of setting targets with pupils is clearly relevant to sharpening up the feedback we give to pupils. It is teachers and tutors who are now urging that targets should not be 'fuzzy' or 'woolly'. In this, they are building on the work of special needs co-ordinators preparing individual education plans (IEPs) for pupils with SEN. 'Learn 5 given spellings a week' or 'Do 20 minutes reading each day' is SMARTer than 'Keep on task', or 'Improve concentration' and 'Improve your presentation'.

Devising SMART targets for 32 pupils across a range of subjects or for anything up to 150 pupils in your own subject can be enormously time-consuming. Increasingly, teachers are working at defining the small steps of progress in advance of setting process targets with pupils. Below are examples of different ways in which teachers are constructing the learning steps that pupils can follow to make progress in a subject.

Breaking down the general targets into SMARTer specifics

Consider, for example, 'Improve your presentation'.

With one or two colleagues, take two or three pieces of work that you would agree are badly presented. Brainstorm in detail what is going wrong, for example:

- not starting exactly at the margin;
- crossing out untidily;
- mis-forming certain letters (be precise: most pupils could improve their handwriting by working at no more than five letters);
- not leaving uniform spaces between words.

Can you collect 20 items? 15? Perhaps you have only identified 10? Fine - but remember to add to them as you encounter more specific causes of poor presentation in your marking.

Now express the same statements as positives, give them to the pupils and ask them to select those targets that are relevant to them.

The advantages of this are:

- the pupils choose their own targets;
- they see that there are things that they are already doing right as well as those they need to improve;
- targets are specific rather than generic.

Use the same technique with 'Participate more in class' or 'Make a larger contribution to class discussion', or whatever your own favoured version of the 'unsmart' target is. A very shy pupil is not going to start contributing to whole-class discussion overnight simply by being given this as a target. What might that pupil do?

- Ask two questions over the course of three lessons.
- Make two contributions in a small-group discussion.
- Make a short presentation to a small group of friends.

Once again, you could brainstorm with colleagues about ten examples so that the pupil can choose one or two. You will notice that process targets are a two-way process between pupil and teacher. The pupil needs to agree what he/she will do as a short-term target. You need to ensure that you have organised activities in which the target can be reached.

Using National Curriculum criteria for levels

Since progress for pupils is often expressed in terms of their progression through the National Curriculum levels, it is understandable that teachers are increasingly sharing level descriptors with pupils in pupil-friendly language. In the example overleaf, teachers from Northumberland Park Community School have listed pupil-friendly level statements for modern foreign languages expressed in terms of 'I can' statements. The statements are kept in the pupil's folder with the pupil able to record their current level.

How would a pupil be able to use this self-assessment sheet to set targets?

Using assessment criteria and exemplars

Consider two of those comments that are the stock-in-trade of many teachers. "You need to develop your ideas" or "Don't copy! Put this in your own words." These can be less than helpful as they refer to quite complex skills. A possible way of short-circuiting a good deal of explanation is to use an exemplar - "This is the sort of thing I meant." Increasingly, teachers are using such examples of grades, marks and levels as part of the teaching process. A team of art teachers regularly display two (unnamed) pieces of work with the clear statement "This piece was awarded a B - this one a D. Can you think why?" To prompt discussion, the teachers then add to the display the four elements that were taken into account in awarding a grade.

"It's all part of understanding the B-ness of B and the D-ness of D!"

A music teacher used the mark scheme on page 41 as part of the teaching in preparation for an exercise in 'Performing a solo piece':

Modern Foreign Languages
National Curriculum: Pupil Self-Assessment - Years 7, 8, and 9 Key Stage 3

Attainment Target 2 - Speaking

Level 1   I can say one or two words in French.

Level 2   I can answer simple questions, describe people and things. I can ask for help from my teacher in French.

Level 3   I can have a short conversation with someone and I can talk about the things I like and don't like.

Level 4   I can make up a longer conversation with someone. I sound a lot more French now.

Level 5   I can have a short conversation asking questions and expressing opinion about what I have done and what I am going to do.

Level 6   I can express views about myself and current affairs. I can cope with a number of unexpected situations and I have good pronunciation.

Level 7   I can cope with a greater number of unexpected situations and use a wide range of vocabulary and more complex sentences. I can speak with confidence, have good pronunciation and make only few errors.

I am now on Level _____ in Speaking (AT2)

Name: _____   Form: _____

Teacher: _____   Date: _____

Modern Foreign Languages
National Curriculum: Pupil Self-Assessment - Years 7, 8, and 9 Key Stage 3

Attainment Target 3 - Reading

Level 1   I can read a short list of words.

Level 2   I can read a short phrase.

Level 3   I can read a short conversation.

Level 4   I can read a short text or story.

Level 5   I can read about the present, past and future in a magazine, brochure or short book.

Level 6   I can read a magazine or short book.

Level 7   I can read a book and use new words in writing.

Level 8   I can read difficult books and understand characters.

I am now on Level _____ in Reading (AT3)

Name: _____   Form: _____

Teacher: _____   Date: _____

Northumberland Park Community School

The piece assessed must be allocated a mark out of 10 using the following indicators as a guide:

1 - 2 marks	The piece is played but with frequent breakdowns. There is an attempt to play the correct pitch and rhythm but with only limited success.
3 - 4 marks	The complete piece is played with some breakdowns but the pitch and rhythm are recognisable.
5 - 6 marks	The performance is coherent but the technical control is not always adequate for the demands of the music.
7 - 8 marks	The performance is reasonably accurate and is partially successful in interpretation
	OR the performance is fluent and technically correct.
9 - 10 marks	The technically correct performance is fluent and expressive and has an appropriate sense of style.

The initial mark for performance of the assessed part (maximum 10) is multiplied by one of the following numbers according to the difficulty of the part(s) performed, giving a maximum mark of 30.

MEG GCSE Music

The teacher went through the mark scheme explaining words like coherent and technical control and interpretation as part of the teaching programme. Pupils were then told that they would perform their solo pieces next week and mark their own work. Imagine the motivation to practise so that there are at worst some breakdowns and not frequent ones!

Systems for setting targets

It may be argued that sharing the means of assessment with pupils and giving pupils specific feedback on what they need to do to improve has always been part of good teaching. However, the process of giving pupils predicted and target grades and then telling them what they need to do to move from one to the other has sharpened up these familiar practices. Many schools have moved to incorporate these processes in a whole-school approach to target-setting with pupils.

The role of the class or subject teacher is clearly crucial. You are the one who can:

- share with pupils the procedures and results of assessment;
- establish with them realistic and challenging outcome targets;
- agree the process targets whereby the pupil can meet the outcome targets;
- ensure that activities are organised which allow the pupil to meet the targets.

The process is outlined in the use of baseline assessments. All LEAs are now required to make such assessments of all pupils in their first term at primary school. These assessments cover the basic skills needed by the child at the start of schooling. While there is no nationally agreed scheme of baseline assessment, most schemes will group assessments under general headings such as 'Personal and social development' and 'Language and literacy skills'. Baseline assessment has two main purposes:

- to provide information for teachers to help them to plan to meet individual learning needs;
- to provide a baseline measure for future value-added analyses.

Teachers who have assessed pupils against these criteria have found it useful to use the following statements as targets for pupils: 'Concentrate on a directed task for at least 10 minutes', 'Use small apparatus appropriately, such as threading beads' and 'Recognise 14 or more letters by shape'.

The advantage here of course is that one teacher has an overview of the pupil's progress across a range of skills. This becomes more difficult at the secondary phase. Nevertheless, subject teachers remain interested in target-setting within their own subject. In the example below, a Maths team invite pupils to assess their progress against statements relating to a National Curriculum level. Targets can be agreed on following the self-assessment process.

Attainment Target 2: Number and Algebra

	Date achieved in:	Class	Test

Level 6

A. I can order and approximate decimals when solving numerical problems and equations such as $x^2 = 20$, using trial and improvement methods. — A ☐ ☐

B. I am aware of which number to consider as 100% or a whole and I can use this to evaluate one number as a fraction or percentage of another. — B ☐ ☐

C. I can understand and use the equivalences between fractions, decimals and percentages. — C ☐ ☐

D. I can calculate using ratios in appropriate situations. — D ☐ ☐

E. I can find and describe in words the rule for the next term or 'nth' term of a sequence where the rule is linear. — E ☐ ☐

F. I can formulate and solve linear equations with whole number coefficients. — F ☐ ☐

G. I can represent mappings algebraically and interpret general features and can represent mappings using graphical representations in 4 quadrants as appropriate. — G ☐ ☐

Level 7

A. When estimating I can round to one significant figure and multiply and divide mentally. — A ☐ ☐

B. I understand the effects of multiplying and dividing by numbers between 0 and 1. — B ☐ ☐

C. I can use a calculator to solve numerical problems involving multiplication and division with numbers of any size. — C ☐ ☐

D. I understand and use proportional changes. — D ☐ ☐

E. I can find and describe in symbols the next term or 'nth' of a sequence where the rule is quadratic. — E ☐ ☐

F. I can solve simultaneous equations using algebraic methods in two variables. — F ☐ ☐

G. I can solve simultaneous equations using graphical methods in two variables. — G ☐ ☐

Monks' Dyke Technology College

The role of the tutor in secondary schools is clearly crucial because they have the overview of the pupil's progress across the subjects, without being an expert in each particular subject.

> "Many secondary schools are setting targets for and with individual pupils. In classrooms, it is usually more practical to set class or group targets. Where there is a strong tutorial system in a school, the tutors can help pupils set individual targets."
>
> DfEE, *From Targets to Action*

The tutor now has access to an enormous amount of information - both qualitative and quantitative - on pupils, which must be made manageable:

- pupils' test scores on entry/baseline assessments;
- predicted grades;
- pupils' self-assessment;
- subject reports;
- teachers' assessments of level/grades.

On the basis of this, tutors can help pupils to set process targets, particularly after reports/profiles have been received. The role of the tutor is to give pupils the necessary prompts that lead to meaningful targets. The process in some schools is like this:

Target-setting
Pupils read profile/report and choose targets in some or all subjects.
Targets are written down - "These are my targets".

Tutor prompts pupils to produce SMART process targets: "To reach my targets, I will do the following things".

Target-reviewing
Pupils review their targets: "Have I met my targets? Yes/no/partly - because ... "

Tutor prompts pupils to secure that achievement: "What do I need to do to make sure I don't have to repeat that target?"

One difficulty with this process is that, as we have seen, some subject reports can contain fairly generalised comments of the 'Improve your presentation' nature. You would not wish, however, to suggest that "Jon is working at forming the letters g and q" is an adequate target for six months, while it may be a very useful short-term specific target for him.

The issue is: How do we combine the roles of the tutor and subject teachers so that the data held by the tutor can combine with the quality of feedback owned by the teacher to help the pupils make meaningful targets, without increasing bureaucracy?

The target-setting schedule overleaf is one example of a school combining the contributions of subject teachers, tutors, pupils and parents. The tutor seeks to focus on targets that would assist the pupil in a number of subjects. The subject teachers give specific subject targets through assessment and marking. The process has the following elements which seem to be common to a number of well-established and successful schemes:

- two reporting points per year;
- a high level of involvement from pupils;
- the system co-ordinates existing school processes rather than adding new ones.

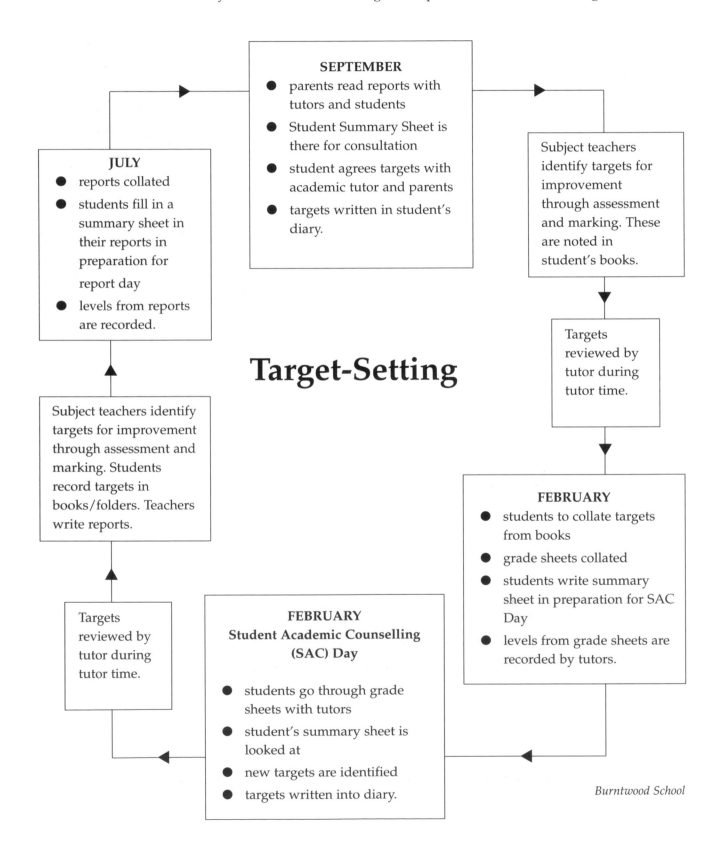

Target-Setting

SEPTEMBER
- parents read reports with tutors and students
- Student Summary Sheet is there for consultation
- student agrees targets with academic tutor and parents
- targets written in student's diary.

Subject teachers identify targets for improvement through assessment and marking. These are noted in student's books.

JULY
- reports collated
- students fill in a summary sheet in their reports in preparation for report day
- levels from reports are recorded.

Subject teachers identify targets for improvement through assessment and marking. Students record targets in books/folders. Teachers write reports.

Targets reviewed by tutor during tutor time.

Targets reviewed by tutor during tutor time.

FEBRUARY
- students to collate targets from books
- grade sheets collated
- students write summary sheet in preparation for SAC Day
- levels from grade sheets are recorded by tutors.

FEBRUARY
Student Academic Counselling (SAC) Day

- students go through grade sheets with tutors
- student's summary sheet is looked at
- new targets are identified
- targets written into diary.

Burntwood School

Setting school and class targets

Setting targets with and for pupils is not part of the statutory scheme, although headteachers and governors have been encouraged to use teacher forecasts as part of the information they use to set the school targets.

Information that headteachers and governors need:

previous years' RESULTS	national and LEA BENCHMARKS
national and LEA AMBITIONS	teacher FORECASTS

From Targets to Action, page 18

Increasingly, the talk now is of the need for 'joined-up thinking' about the levels of pupil performance targets:

National:
What targets should we set ourselves as a country?

↓

LEA:
What targets should we set locally?

↓

Headteachers and governors:
What targets should our school be capable of?

↓

Class teacher:
What targets can my pupils manage?

↓

Pupil:
What targets should I set myself?

We hardly need to demonstrate that these levels of targets are inter-related - and that the class teacher and pupil targets are central. A school may have set some targets for KS1 as follows:

● to raise the proportion of pupils getting Level 2 in reading by 5%;

● to raise the proportion of pupils scoring above 85 in a standardised test to 100%.

These targets must bear a very close relation to the challenging and realistic targets that you have set for your pupils.

Aggregating your individual pupils' target grades into class targets can give both teacher and pupils a sense of shared purpose. At the beginning of Chapter 1, we suggested that you could express your aspirations for your class in a variety of different targets. You might set threshold targets, such as the proportion of your pupils reaching a certain level/grade or above. You might also set reliability targets, for example targets that say "All (or nearly all!) of my pupils will reach at least ... " Reliability targets set out to reduce failure and to establish a minimum entitlement for all of your pupils. They can be the most challenging targets of all.

We have said that target-setting with pupils can raise performance by:

- setting a target of achievement beyond the predicted outcome;
- discussing how that target might be reached.

It would be nice to think that having set and agreed these targets, progress towards them is steady and automatic - but we know it isn't. Prior attainment may account for over 50 per cent of the variability between different pupils' examination results, but there are other factors. Some of these may be highly personal to an individual child; unforeseen and almost beyond our influence. But other factors aren't. Beneath the data on our pupils' performance lie patterns and trends that we need to recognise if we are to do something about them. This is discussed in the next chapter.

Action points

1. Consider three pupils of similar prior attainment. List the factors that might lead you to predict different outcomes for each of them.

2. What measures could you take to counteract specific negative factors such as 'doesn't complete homework' or 'seems to lack motivation'?

3. Look at the levels of performance which you have predicted for your pupils at the end of their current key stage, following your work on Chapter 1. Do these levels reflect 'prediction + challenge' thinking?

4. Make sure that you know your school's practice in setting targets with pupils. How does it compare or contrast with examples given in this chapter?

5. With a colleague, list - if possible in order of difficulty - activities that would be SMART targets for the more general 'making a larger contribution in class'.

6. As you read your pupils' writing, compile a list of rules and practices that would help pupils to improve their spelling.

7. Consider a mark scheme that you have used recently to assess pupils' work. Could you share it with pupils as it is or are there concepts you would need to explain?

8. Make sure that you know the statutory targets your school has set. Would you agree that they are challenging but realistic?

Chapter 3

USING THE DATA

'Data is inert until someone handles it and makes it powerful.'

IBM

> **This chapter looks at using data on pupil performance to decide on future action. It offers help with:**
> ☞ **using data to see how well you are doing;**
> ☞ **using data diagnostically;**
> ☞ **using data to set your own action plans.**

Factors that affect pupil performance

Imagine again that largely well intentioned and groomed new class we read about in Chapter 1. Having read that chapter, you are probably now using your markbook as a simple database in which:

- you have recorded relevant data on your pupils' prior/current attainment;
- you have recorded your predictions of their future performance (in line with your departmental/school assessment policy);
- you will, over the next months, track their progress against predictions and possibly revise those predictions, hopefully upwards.

You may also have set class targets using the format given in Chapter 1. Class targets for a Year 6 class at the beginning of the year might look like this:

- In English, 15 pupils in this class should be working at Level 4 by the end of the year, and 8 pupils should be working at Level 5.
- I hope that the whole class achieves at least Level 3 by the end of the year.

This database that you have created is powerful: when you say that pupils are 'on track', you and they know what the track is. When you write in reports that they are not fulfilling their potential, you, they and their parents have - written down - what you believe that potential to be, based on data on prior attainment.

However, dangers may lurk in the database too. The combination of prior attainment and predicted outcome can lead us all to assume that the pupils - and you - only have to turn up and progress will occur. This is not necessarily the case!

It's obvious but still worth saying - progress isn't automatic, it isn't guaranteed and it shouldn't be constrained by your predictions. Three pupils can begin Year 3 or Year 7 with near identical prior attainment and, three years later, achieve quite different

Chapter contents

■ **Factors that affect pupil performance**

■ **Account-ability and diagnosis**

■ **From review to action**

■ **Case studies**

outcomes - one the predicted outcome, another way above and the other way below. Factors external to school may account for this and be beyond your control. What you can work on are the factors within your control - the quality of teaching and learning within your class. Furthermore, we know that effective teachers and effective schools can work to minimise the effect on pupil performance of factors which are known, on a national scale, to account for much of the variability between different pupils' performance data.

Consider critically two of these factors and tackle certain assumptions that are often made. 'Yes, but ... ' is a useful phrase to use!

Prior attainment

We all know that prior attainment accounts for over 50 per cent of the variability between different pupils' examination results. Yes, but we also know that, nationally, significant numbers of pupils with the highest levels of prior attainment don't go on to achieve five A* - C passes at GCSE whilst, conversely, significant numbers of pupils with the lowest levels of prior attainment do go on to achieve five A* - C passes. In short, as the chances graphs show, all is still to play for. Schools can make a difference. Departments can make a difference. Teachers can make a difference.

Gender

We all know that girls are outperforming boys at school. In 1998, they outperformed boys nationally in the achievement of five or more A* - C passes by around 10 percentage points. They outperform boys in all but one of the 12 most popular GCSE subjects. The situation is just as marked at Key Stage 1. As the table opposite shows, girls outperformed boys in the percentage of pupils achieving Level 2 or above in all aspects of the 1998 Key Stage 1 teacher Assessments/Tasks.

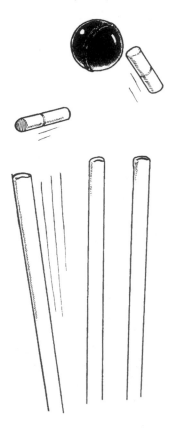

Making Pupil Data Powerful - a guide for classroom teachers

Percentage of pupils who achieved Level 2 or above in:		National results
Reading Test/Task	All	80
	Boys	75
	Girls	84
Writing Task	All	81
	Boys	76
	Girls	86
Spelling Test	All	66
	Boys	60
	Girls	72
Mathematics Test	All	84
	Boys	83
	Girls	86
English Teacher Assessment	All	81
	Boys	76
	Girls	86
Mathematics Teacher Assessment	All	85
	Boys	83
	Girls	87
Science Teacher Assessment	All	86
	Boys	85
	Girls	87

The Autumn Package, 1998, Key Stage 1

It is not surprising if many of the boys in your class have lower scores of prior attainment and therefore lower predicted outcomes. Yes, but, we also know that within these national figures, there are enormous variations between LEAs and, within LEAs, from one school to another. In one LEA, for example, in one year, girls outperformed boys at GCSE by 13.8 per cent on average. But behind that average figure lay huge differences, with a range of 2.5 per cent to 28.2 per cent from one school to another. Once again, schools can make a difference; within schools departments can make a difference; and, within departments, teachers can make a difference.

Concerned and committed teachers have always asked themselves "What difference do I make?" or "What value do I add to my pupils' attainments?" These questions can usefully become the starting point for a systematic approach to raising your effectiveness as a teacher and therefore the performance of your pupils. Looking at the data on our pupils' performance is the first stage of that approach. The problem is that so much data comes into our schools, from so many different sources, in so many different formats and at such different times of the year that it's no wonder we do not make best use of it and that too often it ends up in the filing cabinet! To make best use of it, we need to take an active stance; we need to interrogate the data and we need to distinguish between two types of questions - questions for accountability and questions for diagnosis.

Accountability and diagnosis

Accountability

Questions include:

- How well are we doing as a school/department?
- How do we compare with similar schools/departments?
- Have my pupils made as much or more progress as pupils of similar prior attainment in other classes/subjects/schools?

For these questions, we need contextualised comparative data; data that places our pupils' performance and progress data alongside national benchmarking data showing how pupils in similar schools have performed and - critically - how pupils of similar prior attainment have progressed.

Essentially, data for accountability is descriptive rather than diagnostic. As the word suggests, it gives an account of how you and your pupils have performed. It does not explain why you have performed as you have or suggest what you need to do to make a difference in the future. The danger in the past has been that we have tended to spend too long answering the question "How well have we done?" and have not always moved on to "What do we need to do to improve?" Fortunately, as we saw in Chapter 1, the Autumn Package now provides comparative tables showing succinctly the performance of similar schools, based on the proportion of pupils known to be eligible for free school meals. As national data builds up, it is possible to provide benchmark information on the basis of levels of prior attainment in schools as in the example below from the Key Stage 4 package:

All schools that achieved a Key Stage 3 average level of more than 3.5 and up to 4.0 in 1996

Percentage of pupils	95%	UQ	60%	Median	40%	LQ	5%
English GCSE A* - C	39	29	24	22	19	16	9
Maths GCSE A* - C	33	21	18	16	14	11	5
Science GCSE A* - C	34	24	20	17	15	11	4
5+ GCSE/GNVQs A* - C	34	23	19	18	15	13	6
5+ GCSE/GNVQs A* - G	92	84	79	77	74	69	58
1+ GCSE/GNVQs A*-G	100	94	92	90	88	84	75

Percentage of schools achieving:

	95%	UQ	60%	Median	40%	LQ	5%
GCSE/GNVQ PS 6	33	27	25	24	22	20	16

(number of schools: 254)

The Autumn Package, 1998, Key Stage 4

Diagnosis

Questions include:

- What have I/we done right to improve on the national trend?
- Which aspects of our work do we need to improve?
- Which groups of pupils have done less well than I predicted?
- What are we going to do differently this year to achieve our targets?

A systematic approach to using questions for diagnosis appears below.

Using questions for diagnosis

1. In which areas do the results of my class or subject fit national trends?

    ....

    ....

2. In which areas do the results of my class appear to differ from national trends?

    ....

    ....

3. What aspects of class performance need to be improved?

    ....

    ....

4. Which pupils need specific help and of what kind?

    Name   Support

    ....

    ....

5. Which pupils have done better than expected and why?

    Name   Reason

    ....

    ....

6. What have I done differently this year that has produced different results?

    ....

    ....

7. What will I do differently next year to improve on these results?

    ....

    ....

For these questions, we need data that shows us patterns and trends, data on different aspects of the curriculum and data about the differing performance of groups of pupils. In short, the process of improvement for a school, a department, a teacher or a pupil is another variation on the well-known cycle:

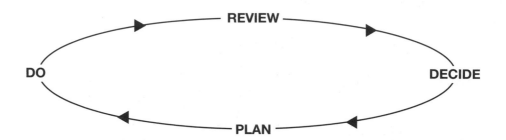

At the end of the process, we reach its purpose - action!

> 'Sooner rather than later, the school should move from reviewing performance to taking action. Sharing an agreed picture of the school's performance and with clear targets for improvement, discussions in the school should turn to action planning.'
>
> *Autumn Package, 1998*

From review to action

Remember that you should:

- be selective;
- be specific;
- move to action.

Being selective

Just consider how much data may come your way in the course of a year, including:

- percentage of pupils gaining each National Curriculum level/GCSE grade;
- percentage of boys and girls at each of the above;
- performance across different subjects;
- performance across different elements of the assessment, e.g. different attainment targets or tasks;
- performance across different teaching groups;
- teacher assessment compared to test scores;
- predicted grades compared to actual grades.

Much if not all of the above can be compared to the same data over the past three years, showing trends over time. It can also be compared to the same data in a national and/or LEA context. Value-added data, showing what progress your pupils have made over a key stage, can also be compared to the national context.

Which of all the data listed above would be most helpful to you?

Making Pupil Data Powerful - a guide for classroom teachers

Being specific

Very often, one piece of data will prompt us to look at extra but more specific data. This is part of taking an active stance towards data. Consider the example below, in which a Year 6 teacher and the Science co-ordinator review the school's Key Stage 2 results, benchmarked against results from similar schools:

SCHOOL NAME							
	High	UQ	+	Med	–	LQ	Low
English							
TA		74	67	60		43	
Test		66	58	50		33	
Mathematics							
TA		73	57	57		39	
Test	65	64		46		29	
Science							
TA		85		70	68	50	
Test		88		75	58	57	

National percentage of 11 year olds in each school achieving Level 4 or above: upper quartile, median and lower quartile. Your school's results are shown in **bold**.

Using Assessment Results (Primary), CSCS

Clearly, the teachers will note that pupils have done less well in science than in English and mathematics. They will also note that the teacher's assessment has been considerably higher than the test results.

What more detailed data would now be useful for those teachers in deciding on a course of action?

Moving to action

Someone once said: "Insanity is doing the same things and expecting different outcomes!" If there's a grain of truth in this, let's pose a deliberately provocative question about the question of what we decide to do:

What are you going to do differently this year to achieve improved results with your pupils; however well they (and you!) have done so far?

Remember the pupil at the beginning of Chapter 2 who knew that she needed to do something different: "If I always do what I always did, I'll always get what I always got."?

Is the same true for you as a teacher? Is the action plan (referred to in the last chapter) that you've put alongside your target for a particular pupil or for your class more of the same or a new emphasis or initiative? What does the data on your pupils' performance suggest you might do differently this year?

Remember that you are looking for patterns. Consider the data on your pupils' performance within your subject or your class and discuss it with a colleague. Ask yourselves two key questions:

- Have some groups of pupils made more progress than others, e.g. girls/boys, higher/lower prior attainment, different ethnic groups? If so, why - and what am I going to do about it?

- Have some parts of our teaching/learning been more successful than others? If so, what are we going to do about the less successful parts?

The answers to these questions will lead directly to action plans.

Have some groups of pupils made more progress than others?

For this, we need value-added data and fortunately national value-added data is becoming increasingly available.

Value-added is a way of measuring the progress made by pupils from one key stage to the next, relative to progress made by other similar pupils. This is normally presented in terms of pupils' distance from a 'regression line' or 'line of best fit' which shows the average progress made by pupils from different starting points. Each pupil's progress is plotted as a point and the line of best fit is drawn to minimise the distance between the points and the line itself. The greater the number of pupils whose results are used to determine the line, the more confident we can be that being above or below it represents important information about pupils' performance.

The graph below compares individual pupils with the school's average progress line. Those above the line have made better than expected progress; those below the line have made less progress than expected.

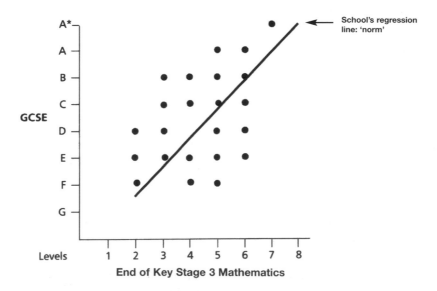

Using Assessment Results (Secondary), CSCS

Pupils achieving the lower levels at KS3 made better than average progress (within the school). What might have caused this? What about the disappointing progress of some pupils at Levels 4, 5 and 6? Are there other patterns here, relating to gender or to pupils of different ethnic groups? Are these patterns new or do they reflect a trend over time? Are these patterns replicated in your class? If not, what is it that you are doing to avoid this school's trend?

Making Pupil Data Powerful - a guide for classroom teachers

We have said before that this is not an exact science. We are dealing with relatively few pupils. However, the advantage is that you know the pupils individually. Are the examples of apparent under-performance all down to individual explanations or can you see a pattern? And is this pattern replicated among pupils nationally?

The following graph shows a school department comparing its progress line with the national line.

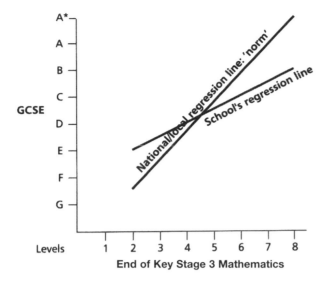

Using Assessment Results (Secondary), CSCS

Pupils with lower attainment at KS3 have progressed better on average than similar pupils nationally, while pupils with higher attainment at KS3 have progressed less well. What might have caused both aspects of this pattern?

The Autumn Package is now giving us 'value-added lines' or 'average progress lines' for pupil progress from KS2 to KS3 and from KS3 to GCSE/GNVQ, based on the average test/task level at the previous key stage.

In the value-added information given overleaf, plotting progress made between different points of attainment at KS2 and attainment three years later, three different rates of progress are shown: the solid line shows the median pupil's Key Stage 3 attainment nationally for any given average Key Stage 2 test-task level. The dotted lines show Key Stage 3 attainment for pupils at the upper and lower quartiles.

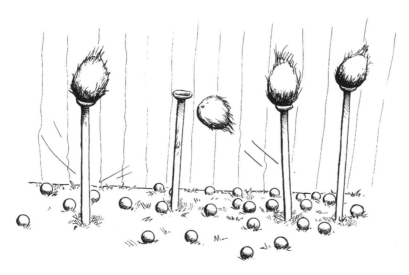

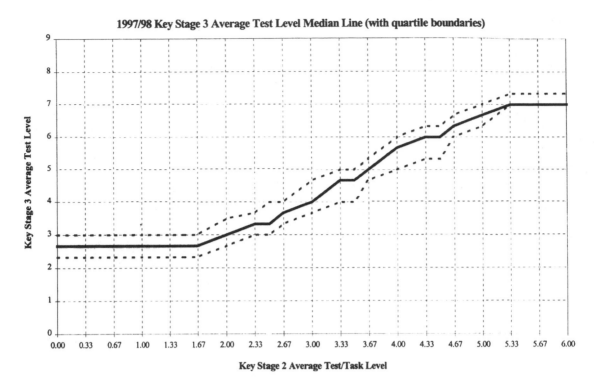

1997/98 Key Stage 3 Average Test Level Median Line (with quartile boundaries)

Y-axis: Key Stage 3 Average Test Level

X-axis: Key Stage 2 Average Test/Task Level

The Autumn Package, Key Stage 3

By plotting onto the graphs the attainment of your individual pupils, the progress they have made can be compared with the progress made by pupils nationally from similar prior attainment. You can also look for patterns relating to gender and/or ethnicity.

Have some parts of our teaching/learning been more successful than others?

This question shifts the focus from our pupils to our own resources as teachers. It should not make us feel guilty, inadequate or affronted. It is very unlikely that we are equally successful across the whole curriculum - and, as with our pupils, we can do something different to improve!

Think of your teaching programme for the next term and ask yourself the following questions:

- Which aspect, unit or skill do I least like teaching?
- Do the pupils generally perform less well in it than in others?
- Am I spending the right amount of curriculum time on it?
- Do I need to re-plan the activities I use with the pupils?
- Do I need different resources?
- Do most teachers feel like this about this aspect, unit or skill?
- Who can I talk to about it?

These may seem very basic questions. However, used regularly and systematically, they become part of the process of using data to inform curriculum planning. It's only human nature that we should spend time on those activities that we enjoy most. Is that true of your practice as a teacher? Do you tend to re-visit and improve your planning for those areas of the curriculum that are already quite effective? Remember the reply of the team coach who was asked the secret of his team's success:

"We practise what we're not good at!"

Increasingly, team coaches are looking with their
players at the wealth of computer- generated data
provided at the end of each match. Teachers too are
generating a wealth of data through assessment. Are
we also finding time to look - hopefully with others - at
what the data is suggesting we could improve in our
own performance as teachers? In their book *Effective
Heads of Department*, Phil Jones and Nick Sparks outline
the process of teachers meeting after setting and
marking a common assessment with a common mark
scheme to look for patterns in pupils' performance:

'Having identified what pupils are expected to know,
understand and be able to do, the assessments a class
undertakes should provide teachers and the
department with sound evidence of how effective a
teaching programme has been. For example, it might be that, having completed a
particular unit, the assessment reveals that there were some aspects of the intended
learning that very few pupils managed to grasp. This in all probability indicates that
there is a need to adjust the teaching programme to ensure that these important features
are covered more effectively. A systematic approach to making assessment work for you
can be a powerful key element of a department's self-review process.'

Case studies

Deciding what action to take following a review of the school's or department's
performance is properly the province of teachers. A word of warning: "Beware the
Boxer syndrome!" Remember the horse Boxer in *Animal Farm* whose motto was "I will
work harder"? Remember what happened to him?

It's not a question of doing more, but of choosing to do what is most likely to make a
significant difference to pupil performance:

> 'Headteachers, governing bodies and teachers need to be very clear-headed
> about what works in raising achievement.'
>
> *From Targets to Action, DfEE*

Looking at data is the first step in that process. The case studies that follow are all
examples of teachers using their own data to decide on what to do differently to raise
pupil achievement.

Case study 1

For the first time, a school had data on its Year 11 cohort of 240 pupils which allowed it
to track progress from:

Year 6 (reading scores) ⟶ KS3 test levels ⟶ GCSE grades

In looking at progress from KS3 Level 5 to five or more A* - Cs, it discovered that:

- All pupils achieving Level 5 in the three core subjects went on to gain five or more A* - Cs at GCSE;

- All pupils achieving Level 5 in English but Level 4 in maths and/or science went on to gain five or more A* - Cs at GCSE;

- Pupils achieving Level 4 in English but 5 in maths and/or science did not all go on to achieve five A - Cs at GCSE.

For this school, Level 5 in English at Key Stage 3 was a clear indicator for success at GCSE, largely because, in so many subjects, in order to perform your understanding of the subject, you need to be able to write at an appropriate length and in appropriate formats.

The school asked all subject departments to look at their own subject data and to see if extended writing was an issue. It was in almost all subjects and was frequently the area in which there was a trend for boys to do less well than girls. Design and technology staff discovered that, almost without exception, boys had performed best in the practical element of their subject and had lost marks in the extended writing. History and music teachers reported that, in the mock examinations, most boys had written shorter, less fluent answers than most girls, although the teachers believed their knowledge and understanding were equal.

Action
The school made supporting extended writing a focus for all year groups. Strategies adopted throughout the school included:

- the use of writing frames/templates in some departments;
- consideration of syllabuses offering a wider range of assessment tasks;
- the use of sentence stems to begin appropriate answers;
- the use of exemplars.

Case study 2:

Looking at their data on pupils' progress through the levels at Key Stage 3, a languages department observed certain patterns, for example a number of pupils found progression from one particular level to another difficult. The team decided to revisit, at first for themselves, what was required at each level, using the level descriptors and exemplar material.

In a brainstorming session, they deliberately used their own words:

Speaking
Levels 1-3:
- narrow range of simple language
- approximate pronunciation
- hesitant
- using memorised language
- beginning to substitute words.

Making Pupil Data Powerful - a guide for classroom teachers

Levels 4-6:

- longer responses
- wider vocabulary
- greater degree of accuracy
- improved pronunciation
- increased confidence
- adapting language
- starting to use different tenses although there may be some inaccuracies.

Action

The next step was to share these perceptions of what constitutes a level with the pupils. Although the details are particular to the languages department, the principle of establishing a shared sense of a level is good practice across all subject areas.

Case study 3:

A geography department set itself the KS4 target of increasing the percentage of pupils gaining A* - C grades from 45% to 55% in three years. Its process for doing this was to continue to develop student study guides covering each unit of the course. Each guide was to identify:

- learning objectives expressed in terms of areas of knowledge, understanding and skills, in student-friendly language;
- a range of activities classified 'must', 'should ' or 'could' and including a variety of learning styles;
- the resources available;
- the nature of assessment and assessment criteria.

Action

This consciously builds on good practice in promoting learning. What is impressive is that the department in question, after a successful pilot scheme, deliberately built good practice not only into the departmental development plan but into an action plan for achieving a measurable target for improvement at Key Stage 4.

Case study 4

In the following example, a primary school set out to use its data to agree a limited number of initiatives. It set out its responses in the following way, which builds on established good practice in strategic planning. However, the school deliberately sharpened up its former practice by:

- emphasising the role of data in identifying the focus for improvement;
- setting a specific, measurable outcome target;
- identifying what will be done differently to achieve the target.

Action

The school set itself some key questions for discussion and planned the following strategy.

Questions for discussion	The school's responses
1. Based on an analysis of the results, which area involving pupil assessment is to be the focus for improvement in the coming year?	1. Reading in Year 2, particularly boys.
2. What are the targets and the timescale?	2. To increase the proportion of children achieving Level 2 to 90% over two years.
3. Whom has the headteacher identified as being responsible for monitoring, reviewing and reporting progress during the year?	3. The English co-ordinator, in consultation with the class teacher.
4. What are the implications for: a) the organisation of pupil learning; b) the deployment and training of staff; c) the allocation of resources; d) the allocation of curriculum time?	4. a) Review of reading material to focus on boys' interest. b) Classroom assistant engaged for 3 terms to work with Years 1 and 2. c) Increase of 100% in special needs budget, by reallocating budget from elsewhere. d) Staff time for reading support increased by 5 hours per week.
5. In what ways can the support of parents and the community be involved. Can we use our Annual Report to Parents or the Annual Meeting to get support?	5. Parents' help enlisted for reading programme by hearing children read and keeping a log. Parents' meeting to launch venture.

Characteristic of all four case studies is the practice of teachers working together to decide what works in raising achievement by looking at the evidence of pupils' successes and failures in learning. These decisions are now part of a concrete action plan with a measurable target for improvement so that the teachers can later evaluate the results of their outcome. This is indeed becoming 'clear-headed about what works' in raising achievement.

Data can seem very inert to classroom teachers - and sometimes potentially threatening. It seems to emanate from outside bodies, QCA, OFSTED and LEAs with the express purpose of making you feel anxious or inadequate or guilty. It is important to remember that the national databank is merely the accumulation of data about pupils' learning in classrooms, including yours!

Action points

1. Consider two of your pupils who are not 'fulfilling their potential'. Can you identify the factors that account for this? Are they entirely external to the school or is there something that you could do?

2. Compare the results of boys and girls in your school in recent end of key stage tests/GCSE with the National Summary Results in Section 1a of the Autumn Package. How did your school's results compare?

3. Which data do you and your colleagues use to answer the accountability question "How well are we doing?"

4. Think of the occasions when you have given specific help to individual pupils. What was the nature of the intervention? How successful was it? Could it be used for other pupils?

5. If 'Insanity is doing the same things and expecting different outcomes', what are you going to do differently in the coming year to achieve improved results with pupils?

6. Think of the year's teaching programme that lies ahead. Which aspects of the curriculum most need your attention?

7. Is 'extended writing' an issue for some or all of your pupils? What strategies are you using or might you use to address it?

8. To what extent have you shared with your pupils a sense of the levels of the National Curriculum?

Chapter 4

CONTINUITY AND PROGRESSION

'Rarely, it seems, has information about what teachers have actually taught and what children have actually learned at the previous key stage been used extensively in planning next steps in learning for individuals or groups.'

Mary James, Using Assessment for School Improvement

> **This chapter looks at the use of data to focus on pupil entitlement and expected progression in attainment. It offers help with:**
>
> ☞ **setting expectations for future pupil attainment and a form of curriculum entitlement;**
>
> ☞ **ensuring progression and continuity in attainment from class to class each year, key stage to key stage, and from school to school;**
>
> ☞ **sources of advice, support and information.**

Chapter contents

■ **Variation in rates of attainment**

■ **Continuity and progression**

■ **Dips in pupil performance**

■ **Data and school transfer**

■ **Practice in schools**

Variation in rates of attainment

Several times already, you may have challenged any suggestion that pupil improvement is continuous and predictable. We began by looking at predicted pupil performance. The National Curriculum expects pupils to progress by one level every two years. Targets are set against national expectations for 2002, with the perceived implication that your pupils' attainment graphs will rise evenly and continuously but many teachers suspect that human behaviour is not quite so predictable or as ultimately successful. Patterns of learning vary between all people. Children and adults do not always develop at such an even pace. Every year in a local school, one of the major banks gives the Dark Horse Award to a pupil who pleasantly surprises everyone by attaining unexpectedly high levels of performance at GCSE. Sadly, you may have experienced parallel disappointment when almost inexplicably a pupil fails to attain even a reasonable level of performance, despite early promise and your best efforts. Ballet teachers and football managers might commiserate with you.

As teachers, we recognise some of the reasons for variation:

- rate and speed of pupil learning will vary, as it will in a child's physical growth;
- the 'chemistry', ability and motivation of class groups will vary from year to year, affecting the progress of individuals within it;
- our strengths as teachers differ from each other, and we come and go between schools, temporarily disturbing productive classroom relationships;
- pupils change schools, frequently producing performance dips in attainment;
- publishing results at two key stages may concentrate minds on the results of 11 and 16 year olds particularly, and unintentionally weaken the attention given to other year groups.

Try the following exercise, admittedly a rough and ready illustration of the point above.

Draw two axes (as follows):

- on the horizontal axis, evenly space the next five summer dates, starting with the coming year;
- on the vertical axis, evenly space each year group, putting the most able potentially in attainment at the top, and in your judgement list the other year groups below in descending order of ability (inevitably, this is crude - but keep going!);
- now identify which of your current groups has performed most closely to the year group which has just left in the previous summer - the last measure of your school's performance;
- draw a horizontal 'baseline' level with that year group;
- now mark the anticipated performance of each of your class or year groups:
  - in relation to this baseline - above or below;
  - in relation to the year in which they leave.

Your illustration should look something like this:

Illustrating comparative strengths of year groups
Current year groups in order of predicted attainment

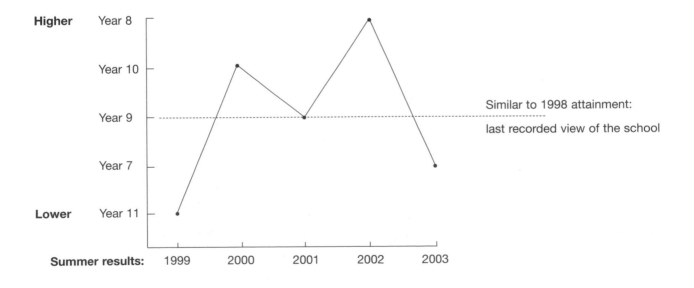

Making Pupil Data Powerful - a guide for classroom teachers

Immediately to the eye, it is apparent that each year group may well perform differently. One or two cohorts will not do as well as your school's class group did last year! The data is available now to confirm or deny your impression of each year group, but each cohort will have its own distinctly different contribution to make to the school's published levels of attainment each year. Be careful not to take this exercise too far. It is merely illustrative of an important point developed below. You will have spotted, for instance, that the perceived differences between year groups will not be as 'equal' as your diagram seems to show.

This may be a useful exercise to share with colleagues, and an aid to understanding for school governors, reasonably expecting steady year-on-year improvement. The need to look at three-year rolling averages for school performance is reinforced by such a diagram. Identifying the three-year average figure will 'flatten' the rises and falls of individual years. It is the reasonable argument that is promoted annually by the Treasury. Never take one year's figures to prove a trend.

It is also a further prompt to you to look closely at where each year group or your class is now and ask "Why is it performing in this way?" It does appear to have developed a unique character in relation to others in this school; sometimes better, sometimes worse. If you can answer the "Why ... ?", you become much closer to knowing what you have to do to improve on the pupils' strengths and to develop the identified weaknesses. Individual year groups and classes require their own customised diagnosis and prognosis.

Continuity and progression

If you know more clearly where your class, subject or year group is now, you also need to know as much as you reasonably can about where you want them to be.

Try this challenge!

Are you now ready to:

- guarantee a minimum level of attainment for the majority of your pupils, recognising the incidence of variation in groups and individuals described above?

- boldly state the entitlement of pupils to expect to make measurable progress, setting out what is the future, measurable 'norm' for attainment in your class, subject or school?

Repeatedly, national concern is expressed about the wide range of pupil attainment at any level of British education, compared with other countries. Professor David Reynolds has drawn attention to the significant 'trailing edge of under-achievement' to be found here. Heady stuff, but as a classroom teacher, can you set out your minimum expectations for most pupils' attainment by the end of the coming year, next year ... and so on? Isn't a pupil entitled to know this? Certainly many parents would welcome the information. We live in a culture of E numbers and product descriptions.

What are some of the risks suggested in these questions?

● The Trades Descriptions Act figures in a mix of humour and seriousness. More informed colleagues refer to a court case in California where the equivalent of an LEA was found guilty of failing its pupils in the quality of its school education. Predicting Lee's future attainment is risky! The risk was identified on the first page of Chapter 1. There is a nightmare vision of Lee's parent appearing in the school corridor, writ in one hand, your school prospectus in the other, but not questioning son's absence on the Costa Lotta holiday!

● A more common concern is that prediction and self-fulfilling prophecy are very similar in the classroom. If Jane is told that she will get Level 4 at the end of Year 6, that is what she will get - and no higher. Jane will work to the level of expectation. It remains important that challenge is an integral part of target setting, and that pupil and teacher look for attainment which improves on prediction.

● You may see worries in predicting levels of achievement, particularly for Teacher Assessment in the intervening years between key stage tests. How sure are you in moderating your own National Curriculum assessments? How confident are you of arriving at agreement with your colleagues? This book sees that as a perceived difficulty which can be turned to opportunity. Everyone benefits if teachers regularly discuss the detail of what is expected at any level or any pupil age. This discussion helps consistency, higher expectations and professional self-development.

Predicting the average pupil's attainment for each year

Within the context of your school, it should be possible to estimate realistically what the 'average' pupil should achieve at the end of each school year and each key stage because:

● you are building a database showing past experience with similar pupils;

● the national and any local benchmark tables will also guide you.

Avoid the time-consuming pedants! "What do you mean by the average child?" Use the growing data of subject assessment to look for a guiding level of achievement which includes approximately the middle 60% of your pupils. Look for agreement on the criteria and particularly the evidence illustrating National Curriculum levels. You are providing a good basis for discussions with colleagues about your collective expectations of pupils' future achievements, their potential in your subject(s) at the end of each year.

Try an example. The exercise opposite is based on Key Stage 3. (A worked primary school KS2 example is available to you on page 35.)

A framework for predicting performance throughout a key stage

1. **Begin by assembling the following data and information:**
   - the benchmarking tables in the Autumn Package, which now take account of prior attainment, and show you how a class with a similar average level of attainment at KS2 might perform at KS3;
   - the chances graphs, also in the school's Autumn package;
   - an understanding of the challenge element of target-setting in Chapter 2.

2. **Add 'in-school' data:**
   - the profile of your class's attainment at end of Key Stage 2 in all core subjects;
   - work out the class average level of attainment;
   - compare this with the relevant benchmark table, and chances graph from the Autumn Package;
   - if available, look at the previous 'track record' of groups in your school at Key Stage 3. (If not available, encourage the school's assessment co-ordinator to build these up.)

3. **Predict the anticipated 'norm' for attainment of your class**
   Use that accumulated information to:
   - estimate how approximately 60% ('the norm') of your class will be expected to perform at the end of Years 7, 8 and 9. Include a degree of challenge!
     Note: Years 7 and 8 will be based on Teacher Assessment Levels only, using the form of differentiation at each level. The Year 9 prediction should be based on the KS3 Test result;
   - estimate how the remaining 40% will perform, placing them in two categories above and two categories below the norm expected;
   - write descriptors for each of the five categories.

Your ambitions for your class in this key stage can be summarised on a table such as this:

Predicting the 'norm' for any group

Attainment descriptors	Predicted end of year levels/grades				
	Y7	Y8	Y9	Y10	Y11
	↑	↑	↑		
	↑	↑	↑		
60% of class or age group	4c	5b	6a		
	↓	↓	↓		
	↓	↓	↓		

Notes:

a) The table is an example for KS3. However, the school could extend it into KS4, giving pupils and parents a stated expectation or 'entitlement' for five years compulsory schooling.

b) The norm for each year end has been set at the level to be expected from approximately 60% of the class. The two categories above and below the line could be left as arrows for the year end, relying on the interpretation of the descriptors by you, the pupil and the parent. You could decide to put in anticipated levels as long as you don't appear to constrain the ultimate attainment of the most able.

c) For the reason above, discuss possible attainment descriptors with other colleagues.

Remember that, at the start of the book, we said that this is not an exact science. Predicting pupil performance has an element of risk, and every one of us improves our skill with repeated experience and a developing confidence, based on good data.

What are the benefits of such a framework?

Continuity and progression in attainment are underlined in a graphic illustration of the way in which a school or a classroom teacher is leading and monitoring continuous improvement. You have made a route map for you and for the class. Whether you are destined to be the Year 4 teacher for years to come, or you are leaving the school in six months, there is a signposted way through the coming key stage(s). You 'begin with the end in mind'.

The OFSTED inspection framework refers to the need to evaluate and report on what pupils achieve, with reference to:

- attainment 'over time, if there are any clear trends ... with a comment on how well any targets set or adopted by the school are being kept';

- 'progress in relation to prior attainment'.

This provides an immediate view on how the individual pupil is progressing. Aggregated, every pupil record provides a view of the class and its progress and continuous development over a school lifetime.

Expectation is made clear. You will decide the extent to which that expectation comes from:

- you alone;

- the agreement of a teacher group including you;

- teacher group discussion, based on external advice and information, such as benchmarking;

- all of the above, plus some form of pupil and/or parent consultation;

- external expectations, including national and/or LEA indicative targets.

The wider the consultation, the more realistic, achievable and challenging becomes the route map destination to all its followers.

Entitlement for pupils is an intended characteristic of our framework. This framework on one side of A4 paper encapsulates a pupil's "What's in it for me?" in terms of attainment. There are no classroom or school guarantees of success for a particular child, but 60-70% (20 out of 30 pupils) will achieve the norm expected. Data shows that this has happened for the last x years. You and your colleagues will be required annually to tweak expectation upwards, but a fair picture of what your class and your school can provide now is there. Classroom achievement is shared and promoted, no-one is misled, and safeguards against that feared writ include continuous monitoring and recorded data of the individual pupil's attainment, motivation and support. The majority will continue to achieve and to improve on their previous best.

The expected variation in pupil learning rates, identified at the start of the chapter, now has some declared boundaries. While not seeking to limit the more able at all, there is now a classroom or school indication of minimum expectation at the end of each year.

Drawing from the earlier list of factors which influence the rate and pace at which pupils improve attainment:

- teachers, pupils and parents can see expected development over a period of more than one year, perhaps ironing out some peaks and dips linked to personal or physical development;
- without too much contrivance, this framework provides a record of 'the possible', the legacy inherited by a group whose 'chemistry' is not as positive in approach as its predecessors: "It has been done before ... this is the expectation";
- new and experienced teachers, pupils and parents have a common marker or map, and temporary teachers see a better context for their work;
- importantly, there is a strong implication that the attainment of all classes and year groups matter. Publication of results at the end of Key Stages 2 and 4 is a pressure, but so often those published results do not reflect what has happened in the preceding years before the one identified.

Dips in performance

You may be aware of the continuing concern expressed about dips in pupil performance, usually said to be evident in Years 4 and 5, and within Key Stage 3. The year of school transfer is a critical point, but there is also interest in the effect each year of the summer holiday and the years in which publication of results is not required.

In February 1999, Her Majesty's Chief Inspector produced his annual report for 1997-98. There are comments on data use, and continuity and progression, which are important for us to know.

In the primary schools' section, there are encouraging comments about current practice:

- 'Schools are making better use of Assessment Data than in the past.' (para. 57)
- 'Teachers are also making greater use of target-setting, for their class, for groups of pupils or for individuals.' (para. 57)

However, in the area which we are looking at now:

- The first paragraph of the primary schools' section reminds readers of one of three major priorities in the previous report of 1996-97: 'particular attention to be given to Years 3 and 4, where progress was weakest.'

- Paragraph 4 of the 1999 report says: 'The variations reported in previous years remain, despite the encouraging trend of rising standards. The greatest gains in knowledge, understanding and skills are still being made by pupils in Year 6 and in reception and nursery classes. The smallest gains are made by pupils in Year 3.'

- 'Pupils' response is good in three quarters of nursery and reception class lessons, in seven in ten Year 6 lessons, but in only six in ten lessons in Years 3 and 4.' (para. 34)

- 'More weak teaching continues to be seen in Years 3 and 4 than in any other years.' (para. 36)

In the secondary schools' section, there is similar praise for the growing use of 'performance data to measure progress and to set realistic yet challenging targets for improvement.' (para. 122). There are also important comments for our attention here. Specifically:

- 'There has been an improvement in the quality of summative ASSESSMENT at Key Stage 3 ... However, the effective use of both effective National Curriculum level descriptions and internal moderation procedures by some subject departments rarely influences practice elsewhere in the school.' (para. 139). Issues of common purpose, continuity and progress must be affected by this variability in practice.

- 'While the quality of SCHOOL RECORDS of pupils' attainment is generally adequate, they often vary in quality within a school. The use of assessment information to monitor progress remains good in about one-quarter of schools but the frequency with which records are updated remains too variable, so that it is difficult to form a judgement of a pupil's attainment and progress other than when reports are being compiled.' (para 140). What is the quality of data and information which you have received about your new class in September?

- 'The TRANSFER AND USE OF CURRICULUM AND ASSESSMENT INFORMATION from primary to secondary schools remains an area of weakness.' (para. 140)

Dips at Key Stage 3 following school transfer

Professor Maurice Galton spoke about his research on school transfer at the annual conference of the Centre for the Study of Comprehensive Schools (CSCS) in October 1997. He compared current practice with his own study of the same Leicester schools between 1975-1980. You may well have anticipated the major change which he reported. Schools now had significantly improved their liaison arrangements, with earlier contact being made between primary and secondary schools, using a range of teaching colleagues, such as deputy heads, subject and year co-ordinators, and specialist teachers for pupils with specific needs. Primary pupils and parents were encouraged to make regular visits to their new school for assemblies, teaching and other activities. He commented more favourably on 'careful and critical documentation and transfer of pupil records', than the Chief Inspector's report above.

Maurice Galton also contributed the following points of interest or concern, which he linked to later dips in performance particularly in Year 8:

- testing of pupils on arrival in the new school had increased since 1975-80;
- there had been few observable changes to teaching styles or the curriculum, and much remained the same, including a dull, administrative first day(s) at the new school;
- a lot of 'starting again' after transfer, not recognising work done in the primary schools (prior attainment), for example, experience in 'fair testing' in primary science not built on at the secondary stage;
- strategies in the new school tending to 'identify problems rather than work to promote continuity';
- 30% of students score less well at the end of Year 7 than at the end of KS2, compared with 40% recorded in the 1975-80 study.

Maurice Galton, John Gray and others at Homerton College, Cambridge, are continuing to explore the reasons for dips in pupil performance.

Data and school transfer

Data shows that attainment dips significantly following transfer between schools. You may feel that this is a problem beyond the influence of the classroom teacher. A study of some of the contributory factors, however, should bring you back centre stage.

Evidence shows that, in some schools, pupils are given work that is set at an inappropriate level in the first few months. Pupils either flounder or mark time. In either case, motivation suffers, with lasting consequences for some. Maurice Galton's study of Leicester schools comments that secondary school teachers tend to focus on identifying problems in new pupils' learning rather than on promoting continuity. As mentioned above, there is evidence of much 'fair testing' in science at primary school, but this is not recognised in the first term of secondary school.

Prior attainment is either not known or not recognised by the new school. Some well intentioned partnerships are guilty of providing information too late after the date of transfer for it to be used in the early, impressionable days of a new pupil's programme. As a classroom teacher, you will need to be determined when finding out if your needed data has arrived at your school. Usually, you can discount the conspiracy theory, aiming to deny you the data. Ends of year are busy, and, often coincide with the period of professional exhaustion.

A tougher nut to crack is the unwillingness of some teachers to take account of prior learning at all! We have already mentioned two possible reasons:

- the desire to give all pupils a fresh start;
- suspicion of any data which we have not generated ourselves.

The effects of the long holiday and strangeness in new surroundings may not be considered when a new pupil's National Curriculum level appears over generous. "The feeder school is inflating its published results ... they don't understand the levels ... ," and so on. It may be that a receiving school subconsciously prefers the starting baseline to be as low as possible if 'value-added' is to be a future significant measure.

Curriculum continuity and classroom methodology are issues requiring separate treatment beyond the scope of this book, but affect attainment on transfer to a new environment. Young people are adaptable, but initial dips in performance are almost inevitable for some. For the moment, they have also lost a large number of positive teacher-pupil relationships.

There are additional administrative concerns, including:

- selection procedures may complicate transfer arrangements, with final destinations for pupil and accompanying records obscured temporarily;

- some schools draw from a large number of feeder schools, with compounded problems in communication with each other.

How can you help with pupil transfer?

It may be that the links between schools are handled mainly or exclusively by your headteacher or more senior colleagues. You are also busy with the current teaching. Nevertheless, the following basic actions are suggested as a help to you in sustaining new pupils' progress, improvement, and self-esteem.

Before you meet the pupils:

- In early July, before September entry for most pupils, keep prompting inside your school for the data on your new pupils (test and confirmed teacher assessment information).

- The year group, subject and SEN co-ordinators with responsibility for the September entry will almost certainly be arranging visits to the feeder schools in June and July. Find out about these visits and the kinds of information being collected, including any samples of your new pupils' work. Be actively interested - it gives additional purpose and support to your colleagues.

- Throughout the year, look for or suggest opportunities to meet colleagues from the feeder phase. Some community partnership schools hold one joint training day per year. Other forms of INSET are usually available regionally, which may help schools which have a widespread catchment area. The immediate purposes might include:

  - discussion on the interpretation of subject levels, building shared sample portfolios of appropriate pupil work;

  - expectations of standards to be reached by the majority of pupils, at any key stage or end of any year, and particularly at the point of transfer;

  - discussion of teaching methodologies, similarities and differences. How can the combined strengths be harnessed to support pupils from 5-18 age range? How can a feeling of continuous learning be promoted?

In September:

● Draw up your basic database of pupil information, with your pupil baseline and prior attainment recorded.

● Make a note of any specific arrangements for individual pupils, such as pupils with special educational needs at both ends of the ability range, or using English as an additional language. There is increasing concern that a dip in KS3 performance may include too many of the most able pupils, whose needs may receive little immediate recognition, losing some impetus and enthusiasm in their first few weeks in a new school.

● From the data, what information can you see about their current knowledge, skills and abilities in your class work? How far can you adjust your schemes of work to recognise their strengths and areas for development? Can you make it clear early on to the class that you are valuing what they have brought with them?

● Be clear about the purpose and implied 'messages' behind any additional screening of pupils' attainment or abilities on arrival in your class. Does the new data add value to what you already know?

● Make your own teaching challenging from Day 1 - and your class administration as discreet as possible.

Everything will not be right first time - but your influence can help your class.

Data's contribution to continuity and progression in the classroom: a checklist for preparing for a new class or year group

● Have I got the minimum data for constructing an attainment baseline, appropriate to the age group of my new class?   Yes/No

● What data is still needed, if any?...

....

● Have I got:

   - recent and relevant examples of all pupils' work?   Yes/No

   - previous teachers' indication of special needs for the less able?   Yes/No

   - ... and for the more able?   Yes/No

● Have I got a good understanding of the relevant basic work done during the pupils' previous year, for example read a copy of their schemes of work?

....

● What are the more challenging or sophisticated areas of work, or approaches to teaching and learning experienced by some/all of my class?

....

....

● The crunch! How do I now intend to apply the knowledge of this data and information to my teaching and the class learning?

....

....

....

● How are the most able going to continue to be challenged and extended?

....

....

....

● How are the least able going to receive additional help?

....

....

....

Practice in schools

It is interesting to look at practice in schools, particularly at the point of transfer between schools. First, middle and upper schools in three-tier systems face issues of continuity and progression between key stages, and you could look at nearby practice if this is available.

Case Study 1:   Transferring information at KS1/KS2

Felmore Infant School, Basildon is using its own A4 size Record of Achievement Folder to transfer information on each child to Felmore Junior School. Basic information on name, address, date of birth and Key Stage 1 data is passed on disk to the Junior School, but most of the pupil performance information is carried in the REACH file. The cost of the pupil files is shared equally by the partner schools.

Baseline information in the pupil's REACH file includes:

● an assessment book completed by the parent (of the child's likes/dislikes, basic skills, etc.);

● an assessment done in the playgroup which feeds the infant school;

● an assessment in school based on the Essex Early Years scheme.

Data and information collected during Key Stage 1 is included in the file:

● SATs results and the pupil's test papers;

● the pupil's reading record book;

● reading scores based on the Birmingham Reading Assessment Scheme;

● all current exercise books;

● other evidence of curriculum work, including photographs of outcomes. (The school tries to ensure that there is evidence which covers the total range of learning.);

● the beginnings of pupil-kept records in PE, art and music, where pupils record their own progress, usually by colouring symbolic drawings, picturing achievement in these areas;

● the school's Home-School communication booklet, which is largely based on reading but is a good contact with parents;

● the termly Consultation Slips, recording formal and informal meetings with parents, summarising outcomes;

● a copy of the annual report sent to parents;

● other information including social skills, personal development etc.

The infant school headteacher commented:
"The infant school has developed its own record-keeping system and 'database'. Little information or systems for record keeping are inherited. Our junior school teachers are encouraged to come and observe pupils at work here. From playgroup onwards, children are encouraged to visit the junior school for assemblies and concerts. In the last term of Year 2, children visit their new class teacher and classroom regularly, and complete a piece of work in the junior school."

Case Study 2: Helping the least able to cope when changing schools at KS2/KS3

Bicester Community College has gained a reputation for working well with its primary partnership group for many years. In common with others, standards of literacy and numeracy provide the focus for action, particularly for pupils transferring schools at the age of eleven. There has been a long-standing concern to raise the standards of the least able, to reduce what Professor David Reynolds calls 'the trailing edge of under-achievement'.

The school is particularly pleased with two features of the local working partnership of schools:

- Together, teachers have identified 30 pupils for each of the summer's literacy and numeracy programmes, lasting two weeks in early August. Parents are very supportive and the children engage in programmes which improve basic skills, by working on themes such as writing a newspaper. A presentation is made by the pupils to their parents. Two other schools in Oxfordshire offer similar opportunities. The school is 'delighted with the results', particularly with the gains in September, ensuring a positive start to the pupils' secondary school career. Parental support is secured at a crucial stage and relationships forged with pupils who lack self-confidence and self-esteem.

- Bicester is using its role as a technology college to promote the use of *Success-maker*, an American computer program designed to improve literacy and numeracy. The school started with two machines; now it has 16, which are available to all pupils, but the less able have priority access and the support of specialist staff. The graded, integrated learning program assesses students' skills and knowledge, moving pupils on to the next ability level when appropriate. Again, the school reports significant gains for pupils who find English and mathematics difficult. Assessment data records gains of up to two years in the reading ages of pupils, who have had access to the machines for 20 minutes per day, for a period of six months.

Case Study 3: Maintaining the momentum in Year 8

(from 'All-in Success', Vol.10, No.1, pages 10 & 11, Winter Edition, 1998-9, of the journal of the Centre for the Study of Comprehensive Schools, University of Leicester)

William de Ferrers School, Essex reported on its involvement in the IQEA project, 'Improving quality education for all', led by Cambridge University's School of Education. Looking specifically at concerns relating to attainment in Year 8, particularly by boys, its author, Keith Sharp, argues that consistency is the key to maximising pupil potential. The school's survey involved the views of 585 pupils and identified three areas for encouraging more consistent practice, on which the article gives more detailed information:

- homework;
- the rewards and merit system;
- the assessment and feedback about pupils' work.

'Consistency of approach is one of the key messages that has emerged from our research on Year 8. ... The outcomes may appear obvious, but if they are not being applied consistently they will be of little effect.'

Case Study 4: Transferring science information during KS3

Bungay High School, Suffolk produced a Liaison Booklet 1999-2000, setting out a programme of structured contacts between partner schools, and with the parents in the catchment area. It also includes specific advice for the transfer of data and other information for all National Curriculum subjects. The science entry illustrates this:

Transfer of records:
- date for transfer of documentation: on or before June 25 1999;
- mechanism: documents to be delivered to KS3 Co-ordinator;
- documentation to include:
    - standardised examination results (including copies of examination papers and mark schemes);
- teacher assessments to include:
    - end of topic test results for ATs 2, 3 and 4;
    - assessment for AT1 using common investigations during Years 7 and 8;
    - confidential reports;
    - a selection of AT1 assessments (about 12) from pupils at different levels.

Consistency of standards

An identical portfolio for this purpose should be maintained in each of the partner schools and contain:
- the level descriptors which should be used as a guide to the expected standards of pupils' performance;
- reference sets of KS3 tests and mark schemes to give a further indication of the standards required;
- exemplar material as provided by QCA;
- exemplar pupil material for Experimental and Investigative Science. This will be annotated to indicate how it provides evidence of attainment of:
    - planning experimental procedures;
    - analysing evidence and drawing conclusions;
    - obtaining evidence;
    - considering the strength of the evidence.
- additional material as developed.

Standardised examination

All pupils in Year 8 take a standardised examination, the content of which has been agreed by the feeder schools. Papers are marked to a common mark scheme, and the results made available to the Upper School.

Action points

1. Become familiar with content and uses of data in Sections 1b and 1c of the school's Autumn Package.

2. Predict the anticipated level of attainment for approximately 60% of your class, subject or year group:
   - for the end of this school year;
   - for the end of the next two or three years.

3. See if you can secure the agreement of your colleagues with parallel classes to your predictions for the coming year(s).

4. Work out the maximum and minimum attainment entitlements for your most and least able pupils, given the data you have.

5. Decide on the actions you (and your colleagues) will take to minimise dips in performance following change of class, teacher or school.

6. Make a list of the curriculum coverage already experienced by your pupils. Decide how will this be reflected in your teaching.

7. Respond to the questions on page 74.

8. Read the appropriate primary or secondary section of the Chief Inspector's report for 1997-98. (www.ofsted.gov.uk)

Chapter 5

CREATING A CLASSROOM CLIMATE FOR LEARNING

'If I had the teaching of children up to seven years of age or thereabouts, I care not who had them afterwards.'

A Jesuit divine

> **This chapter looks at the use of data to promote a climate for classroom learning. It offers help with:**
>
> ☞ **creating and communicating your expectations of the behaviours of the learner;**
>
> ☞ **encouraging pupils to identify with the agreed class or school expectations of the learner;**
>
> ☞ **gaining parental and wider interest in cultivating a positive climate for learning.**

Developing the 'whole child'

Chapter contents

■ **Developing the 'whole child'**

■ **Learning behaviours that improve attainment**

■ **OFSTED and pupil response**

■ **Learning behaviour that supports personal development**

■ **Pupils' contribution to school data.**

We have all met the quotation above in some form, believing that as much as 50 per cent of a child's development occurs before the age of seven. Secondary school teachers may not want to see the inference and application of such thinking, and heavily weighted per capita funding going to Years 1 and 2 in our primary schools! It might also question the recent growth of mentoring schemes at Key Stage 4, when we know that one of the highest correlations in educational research is that between Key Stage 3 results and GCSE grades. Mentoring will help a number of pupils over the Grade C/D divide, but would greater improvement be made by more effective use of the same energy and resources in Year 7? The Jesuit would have mentored much younger pupils.

We assume that the priest was more interested in developing a child's healthy attitude to learning than in recording data, and achieving his Order's performance targets. Good habits are part of learning! In an age of target-setting that is rooted in measurable attainment, there are understandable concerns about the needs of the 'whole child'. Nobody challenges the need for high achievement in any subject, but pupil performance in school is seen as embracing a wide range of behaviours which contribute significantly to effective climates for learning and personal development. For the purposes of this chapter, we will look at two particular areas, keeping an eye on OFSTED expectations in relation to pupil response:

- learning behaviour which is perceived generally as supporting improved subject attainment;

- learning behaviour which is thought to support personal development, and to have a beneficial effect, encouraging a positive pupil response.

Experience and tradition suggest that the school climate for learning is improved if there are opportunities for school-based extra-curricular activities and visits; effective policies for devolving trust, responsibility and initiative to pupils; and active participation by school community interests, such as parents, businesses, organisations and others. These are examples of contributions which many teachers and parents will see as important in developing the 'whole child'.

Learning behaviours that improve attainment

Whatever the focus, school training days often include comments about pupil behaviour. A fresh approach to teaching and learning initiatives has to convince the whole staff that it will work 'with our type of child'. Instantly for some colleagues, there is a mental vision of a wet and windy Friday afternoon, 33 pupils and no ancillary support that day for the three pupils with special educational needs in the class.

Frequently, governors and teachers identify a variety of school activities which are 'barometers' indicating the learning climate in schools:

- attendance figures;

- participation in extra-curricular activities;

- number of exclusions;

- particular skills in music, ICT, and sport;

- parental attendance at progress evenings;

- contributions to the community;

- incidents of vandalism;

- use of national award schemes, such as the Duke of Edinburgh and Youth Awards Schemes.

You could add to this list of indicators.

Classroom expectations

At the start of Chapter 1, we asked you to look at your new class in September. The challenge was to 'begin with the end in mind'. What are your expectations now for this class or year group in twelve months time?

- What should they know and be able to do in classroom work?

- What kinds of positive learning behaviours are to be developed further?

- What kinds of good social behaviours do you hope to see?

Does this all seem a bit 'airy-fairy'? What do you expect to see pupils actually doing in order to satisfy the first and second expectations above?

Good learning behaviours

Try this yourself or with others:

The results in English, mathematics and science may well be improved significantly if all pupils:

- attend regularly;

- come with the right equipment;

- listen and talk in the classroom, respecting the contributions of others;

- question positively and develop a spirit of enquiry;

- share and contribute ideas and resources;

- complete tasks in preparation for the next step;

- enjoy being together and helping each other;

- aim for best performance for a high proportion of the time;

- have strong feelings of self-worth, but also value the worth in others.

Can you suggest three more:

1. ....
....
....

2. ....
....
....

3. ....
....
....

Study skills and attitudes

Effort shown through:	++	+	-	- -
Preparation for lessons	Almost always well prepared with equipment and resources needed for lessons	Usually well prepared with equipment/ resources needed for lessons	Sometimes forgets equipment/ resources	Frequently forgets equipment/resources; inadequately prepared
Identifying targets	Keen to be fully involved in identifying areas of strength/ weakness and to set appropriate targets; individual and thoughtful involvement	Willing to identify areas of strength/ weakness and to set appropriate targets	Sometimes unwilling to identify some areas of strength/weakness and to set appropriate targets	Shows little interest in learning from experience, in identifying areas of strength/weakness and in setting targets
Working on targets	Keen to assess own progress against targets; actively asks for advice and guidance on improving own learning	Sometimes refers back to targets and identifies progress in achieving them	Tends to give up on targets if the 'going gets tough'! Not working on personal targets	Shows very little evidence of perseverance in reaching targets
Commitment to learning	Individual and thoughtful involvement; willing to complete extra work or research; consistent attempt to develop skills and understanding	Positive approach to learning; willing to contribute to all class activities; follows instructions	Not fully committed to learning new knowledge and skills; tends to do the bare minimum required	Unco-operative approach to learning in class; does not respond well to advice on learning; negative approach to tried teaching strategies
Working with others	Contributes constructively and thoughtfully to group tasks; interacts well with all members of the group, showing empathy and understanding	Contributes constructively to group tasks; interacts reasonably with most members of a group	Does not always contribute to group tasks; does not always interact with other members of the group	Unco-operative in working with others; can create problems when interacting with others
Perseverance in tasks	Always on task; tasks completed	On task most of the time; tasks usually completed	Does not settle to tasks quickly; sometimes distracted and off task; time not used appropriately	Frequently off task; much prompting needed; gives up too quickly when finding the work difficult
Personal organisation	Always keeps a full record of work set, attempts the highest possible standard; submits work on time	Records work set; attempts homework; hands in work regularly on time	Work record not regularly kept; tasks sometimes incomplete or forgotten	Work rarely satisfactory, often forgotten and homework completed to a poor personal standard

Developed by Ashcombe School, Surrey

Ashcombe School in Surrey is an over-subscribed comprehensive school with above average results. This can be seen in the character and range of current expectations in the descriptors produced by the school (see opposite). It is a good model which you could easily adapt for your class, subject area or the whole school. A very important element would be the creation of such a table. Ideally, it should result from wide discussion by all classroom participants, aiming at a shared sense of ownership. It certainly focuses the mind on climate and consistency in teacher-pupil approaches to learning.

The school has looked at categories of effort shown in areas of learning behaviour such as:

- preparation for lessons;
- identifying targets;
- working on targets;
- commitment to learning;
- working with others;
- perseverance in tasks;
- personal organisation.

Each category is then described in four stages of development from the least satisfactory forms of response, to the most positive in this school. Your school or your class may have a different starting point or priorities.

For example, a Southwark school recently considered including a line recording the in-house use of four stages in the mastery of many pupils' additional language - English.

Schools with migrant populations might look at ways of acknowledging the importance of full attendance.

Collecting data

Summary of class study skills and attitudes

++	+	-	- -
Zara	Natalia	Lee	Kevin
George	Peter	Diana	Tracy
Asif	Polly	Fatima	Imran
Dale	Saeed	Morgan	Jon
Chloe	Daisy	Kerry	
Kurt	Ian		
David	Christopher		
Bevan	Nicholas		
Emma	Maurice		
Paula			

The Ashcombe School table is constructed to allow for quick assessment of attitudes and behaviours in a class, a year group, or whole school. The data is collected on a form similar to this.

The benefits:

- Such a breakdown, with its quick, crude form of analysis, can produce a picture of where your class, year or subject group are in terms of adopting some of the commonly sought attitudes and behaviours that assist learning.

- The language used to describe the categories will have resulted from teacher discussion as a minimum, but may well have included pupils and perhaps parents. A picture of shared class or school expectations in clear, understandable language will help everyone, including Zara, to appreciate her own strengths, and specific behaviours which Kevin needs to adopt if he is to improve.

- You have agreed expectations, capable of consistent interpretation and expressed in the language of the classroom.

Gaining parental support for classroom expectations

More formal attempts have been made in recent years to harness the help of home and the community in raising classroom achievement. Schools have worked hard to produce resources for pupils, parents and others which set out expectations and forms of support for the learner, including :

- school mission statements/expectations;
- published syllabuses and schemes of work;
- identified learning skills;
- identified achievement and learning targets;
- consultation evenings and 'surgeries';
- pupil and parent subject workshops;
- home-school agreements/contracts;
- homework and revision clubs.

You may wish to add some more of your own:

....

....

Home-school agreements

Home-school agreements are more widely recognised as good practice, and the 1998 Standards and Framework Act places a responsibility on school governors to promote these. The Act proposes that such an agreement includes:

- the school's aims and values;
- the school's responsibilities towards pupils of compulsory school age;
- the responsibilities of parents;
- the school's expectations of its parents.

Again, the quality of the discussion between you and colleagues, and with parents, will have a significant effect on the contract's adoption by everyone and its future success.

Two examples are included of schools' attempts to write a pupil-teacher agreement and a home-school contract.

Teacher and pupil expectations of each other

Staff expectations of students

All teachers and tutors expect students to:

- act politely and with consideration towards themselves and all adults and students in the school;
- listen when teachers/tutors/other students are talking and respect other points of view;
- respond co-operatively to instructions;
- move sensibly and purposefully around the school;
- ensure that they are always equipped with the necessary materials for their lessons;
- to do their best at all times and to take pride in their work;
- follow the school's Code of Conduct at all times;
- take care of the buildings and all school property;
- be punctual at all times;
- complete homework;
- make it as easy as possible in class for every student to learn and for the teacher to teach;
- ensure they use their personal school diary to record all aspects of their work within the school;
- ask if they need help;
- behave in a way in and out of school that contributes to the school's good reputation.

Student expectations of staff

All students can expect teachers and tutors to:

- arrive on time;
- talk to them politely and with consideration;
- treat them as individuals;
- help them to achieve;
- provide support, guidance and advice;
- treat them fairly;
- listen to them;
- outline the programmes of work that they will be following;
- teach appropriate and relevant work;
- give regular feedback;
- set and return homework regularly;
- treat them with respect;
- be interested in their progress and welfare.

At the beginning of each year, students can expect the following information, concerning the programmes of work which they will be following:

a. a course outline for the year on a termly basis;

b. the method/style of assessment to be used;

c. key dates relating to assessment procedures.

'All in Success', CSCS, Vol. 5, No.1, Pages 17-18
'Quality Assurance at Van Dyke Upper School, Bedfordshire'

The lists of teacher and pupil expectations on page 85 are from a secondary school in Bedfordshire, and are the product of asking teachers and pupils about their expectations of each other. The thinking of each group is clear, but it is interesting that the pupil expectations seem more crisply expressed. Ask yourself if you feel that your own class has a clear understanding of your expectations. How, and how far, are expectations made explicit? How much do you rely upon your own behaviour to be an example in the classroom? Most teachers probably employ a mix of the explicit and the modelling.

A primary school example, taken from DfEE case study evidence of home-school contracts, is also included below.

Home-School Contract

The school will:

- encourage children to do their best at all times;
- encourage children to take care of their surroundings and others around them;
- inform parents of the children's progress at regular meetings;
- inform parents about what teachers aim to teach the children each term.

Teacher's signature

The family will:

- make sure the child arrives at school on time - **8.55 am** for juniors, **9.00 am** for infants;
- make sure the child attends regularly and provide a note of explanation if the child is absent;
- attend open evenings to discuss the child's progress, one each term;
- where possible, attend achievement assembly when own child has been chosen.

Parent's signature

The child will keep the school's golden rules:

- I will take care of the equipment and the building;
- I will walk inside the building;
- I will talk quietly;
- I will be friendly;
- I will keep my hands and feet to myself;
- I will be helpful.

Child's signature

Together we will:

- tackle any special needs;
- encourage the children to keep the school's golden rules;
- support children's learning to help them achieve their best.

All Saints' C of E Primary School, Wolverhampton

Promoting expectations of learning behaviours: School practice

Think about your own and the school's practice.

As far as you, the class teacher, are concerned, what school practice is most effective in helping you and your pupils to learn and improve performance? What is least effective?

Most effective practice	Least effective practice
....	....
....	....
....	....

Personal practice

....

....

Measurable data on improvement

Some of the criteria in home-school agreements is in a form which is capable of accurate measurement of its effectiveness when implemented. There are aspects which can be measured objectively:

Staff expectations

- incidents/cost of vandalism
- punctuality
- completed homework (and on time?)
- use of homework diary

Student expectations

- teacher punctuality
- outline programmes of work
- give regular feedback
- set and return homework regularly

We are not arguing that an ability to measure the measurable will add much to implementation, but it will give a better indication of the practical effectiveness of the criteria. There is a danger that the remaining criteria contribute to a worthy 'wish list', with a potential for varied interpretation by teachers, pupils and parents. It matters that you do engage with colleagues, and with pupils and parents, to agree the interpretation of the words which are set down.

As a class teacher ...

I will monitor one aspect of pupil behaviour for a month at a time.

Monitoring this month will involve checking ....

(attendance? prompt return of homework? punctuality? use of library books? other?)

Number in class: ....

Week 1: Number/percentage of pupils completing homework on time: ....

Week 2: ....

Week 3: ....

Week 4: ....

Week 5: ....

Average number/percentage this month: ....

In six months time: ....

The criteria for your observations in less definable areas of pupil response will become clearer as you gain experience. 'Trial and error' has to be recognised when beginning to build data of this kind. The OFSTED Handbook is useful and some advice is included in the next section. Remember too that you do not necessarily have to engage in activity of this kind every month. Choose two aspects of behaviour which merit attention, and measure these at different points in the year.

OFSTED and pupil response

There are at least two good reasons why you should read the OFSTED Handbook, and in particular Section 4, which should be available in your school:

- On page 60 in the current primary, secondary and special school editions, OFSTED sets out advice on how inspection judgements should be made about pupil response. It is helpful to read these and the more detailed observations which follow.

- Defining behaviour in a way which can allow you to measure degrees of improvement is not easy. The handbook helps with some of the words and phrases for the criteria for good learning behaviour. If you attempt to produce a guide for your class, this OFSTED section helps with prompts and vocabulary. It also provides an agenda for discussion with others.

The handbook looks at the responses of pupils, setting out guidance for the inspection of schools.

'Judgements should be based on the extent to which pupils:

- show interest in their work and are able to sustain concentration and develop their capacity for personal study;
- behave well in and around school, and are courteous and trustworthy and show respect for property;
- form constructive relationships with one another, with teachers and other adults, and work collaboratively when required;
- show respect for other people's feelings, values and beliefs;
- show initiative and are willing to take responsibility.'

On the following three pages in the handbook, each of these criteria is examined in more detail. There are examples of types of behaviour, which provide markers for and help in trying to make a judgement about how pupils are responding.

Explore the first of the bullet points above. In your judgement, do your pupils normally show interest in their work? Do you think that they are able to sustain concentration and extend their capacity for personal study? Using the language of the handbook, try the questions overleaf. Apply the inspection grading scheme to give you a firmer purchase on your thinking.

Pupil response assessed by OFSTED grading scheme

Grades:

1. Excellent

2. Very good   pupils show positive attitudes and behave very well

3. Good

4. Satisfactory   pupils behave well but their attitudes to learning are neither
   particularly positive or negative

5. Unsatisfactory

6. Poor   pupils show negative attitudes to learning and there are examples of
    poor behaviour

7. Very poor

Question	Grade	Evidence
1. How good is their concentration in listening to you?		
2. How confidently do your pupils generate ideas and solve problems?		
3. How good is their capacity to persevere and complete tasks when difficulties arise?		
4. How good is their ability to select and use relevant resources?		
5. How great is your class's desire to improve their work and their pride in the finished product?		

Note:

● If possible, ask a colleague to observe your lessons to see if their judgements are similar to your own.

● If you record your observations/grades mid-term, three times per year, you have some crude data on which you can measure progress in pupil response.

● The evidence may be difficult to describe at first. But the observations provide the language with which you can more accurately discuss a pupil's progress with colleagues and parents.

● Using the OFSTED model should give you confidence to be well prepared for any inspection, and make you fully aware of your class's strengths and weaknesses. There should then be few surprises for you in the inspection report.

Learning behaviour that supports personal development

It is useful to look at the work done by Birmingham LEA in this area. Good ideas are often the most simple and direct, but the thinking behind them is the product of many minds, much experience and a bit of inspiration.

In 1997, Birmingham LEA put practical proposals for measuring aspects of a child's development into what it called a 'Guarantee' for its pupils. Expectations were set out for three different phases of 5-18 education. Within an age phase, on one side of A4, the three categories described:

- the contribution of leadership and management to the successful achievement of the two sets of targets below;

- process and experience targets offered to every child in the Authority's schools at the appropriate age;

- the form of the measurable subject targets expected of each of the age-related phases.

When you are 'beginning with the end in mind', this format should help to clarify your expectations for any group of children.

'Processes and experiences'

Birmingham LEA's proposals for schools are shown below. Their inclusion is intended as an illustration and prompt to your own thinking.

Early years
- Parents are their child's first educators. Materials are to be produced which provide parent/carers with many ideas for supporting their child's learning in the early years.
- The magic of story, jingle and rhyme - 1,000 stories to be heard or read together; 100 musical tunes and jingles to be sung; 10 nursery rhymes to be shared and memorised.
- Leading to Reading projects - all children under 5 to have an opportunity of participating in a 'Leading to Reading' project.
- Caring and sharing - every under-5 child to have an opportunity of undertaking a visit and/or an environmental project.
- Expressing and showing - each under-5 child to have an experience in a range of expressive arts and physical activities.

Primary
- Every primary child will have a residential experience.
- Every 6 and 9 year old child takes part in a 'public performance'.
- All 10 year olds carry out an environmental project.
- All parents of 6 and 8 year olds will be told what their child is particularly good at in the expressive arts and be encouraged to provide support.
- Each class of 10 year olds in groups of 5 or 6 will write a story, illustrate it, turn it into a book and present it to five year olds.

Secondary

- By the age of 12, each pupil should have had the opportunity to take part in a literary performance.

- By the age of 13, each pupil should have been involved in an activity which utilises IT skills and is demonstrable to parents.

- By the age of 14, each pupil should have had the opportunity to be involved in an artistic performance or physical activity involving the community.

- By the age of 14, each pupil should have been encouraged to self-monitor their 'health and fitness' profile.

- By the age of 15, each student should have had the opportunity to celebrate languages by using their knowledge of a European or Community language to support others.

- By the age of 15, each pupil should have had the opportunity for an out of school challenge involving self-organisation.

- By the age of 16, every pupil should have participated in a quality work experience placement as part of a planned programme of work-related activities.

- Throughout their total 11-16 school life, pupils should have been encouraged to celebrate the city's wide range of culture and religions and have been taught to promote racial harmony, tolerance and justice.

- Post-16 students should follow courses which reflect their academic and vocational experiences and previous achievements, and have a good chance of achieving their objectives.

Birmingham LEA

Setting targets of 'process and experience'

Identify the class, year group or key stage for whom you are identifying similar processes or experiences, contributing significantly to personal development.

Briefly, describe the processes and experiences which should be part of a pupil's school life during the coming year(s) or key stage.

Identify the kinds of support which you, your subject area and/or your school can provide additionally to ensure that the processes and experiences are enjoyed by all the pupils.

Chosen class, year group or key stage	Processes and experiences	Support to be provided

Setting process or experience targets:

- is part of creating a school culture which encourages learning;

- shows evidence of school values;

- provides a practical response to the variety of preferred learning styles;

- focuses our minds as teachers on achievable and realistic goals.

The third part of the Birmingham Guarantee includes the measurable outcome targets set for the three phases. Your own LEA will have agreed subject outcome targets for the coming two years with your school. The Birmingham proposals for this section, written for all LEA schools, are shown below and the model is adaptable to your class, subject area, year group or school.

Early years
Through the City Education Department's Baseline Assessment for Nursery Schools/Units and Reception classes, to monitor the percentage of children at the respective developmental stages:

- with respect to language and literacy experience:
  1. speaking and listening
  2. reading
  3. writing

- with respect to mathematical experience:
  1. number
  2. algebra
  3. shape and space
  4. handling data.

Primary
- Each school will audit at age 7, 11 and 12 the percentage of:
  (a) apprentice readers
  (b) foundation readers
  (c) advanced readers
  (d) independent readers

and agree targets for decreases in (a) and increases in (c) and (d) over the years ahead.

- Each school to audit at 7, 11 and 12 the percentage of:
  (a) apprentice mathematicians
  (b) foundation mathematicians
  (c) advanced mathematicians
  (d) independent mathematicians

and agree targets for decreases in (a) and increases in (c) and (d).

Secondary
- At the age of 12, every pupil will have their level of attainment in mathematics and reading audited by the school and be offered whatever support is necessary to develop their skills further.
- Each school will have self-generated targets of improved performance in the core subjects at the end of Key Stage 3.

- Each school will attempt to improve their examination results against previous best performance.
- By the age of 16, every pupil should have produced an accredited record of attainment which incorporates a career plan and an IT-driven project.
- A successful transition will be attempted for each pupil to the next stage of continuing education or training/employment.

Birmingham LEA

You can set measurable outcome targets in just the same way as you did for targets of process and experience.

Setting outcome targets for subject achievement provides:

- a more accurate prediction of a pupil's potential;
- a specific focus for measuring a pupil's progress;
- a challenge for teacher and pupil.

Collecting data

It is possible to measure progress towards pupil targets for personal development. Your own class 'process and experience' targets might look like this in September, and be capable of reasonably accurate measurement in the following July:

Class targets for personal development

Personal development targets set in September	Number of pupils achieving the targets in the following July (or %)
Each pupil will be given the opportunity to:	
1. explain a new subject concept to a group of peers, showing a good level of understanding;	
2. interview an adult, produce a recorded or written result, and write to thank the adult;	
3. work in a team to produce an activity in which others take part;	
4. access and retrieve information from the Internet to illustrate personal classroom work.	
Now add some targets for your class:	
5.	
6.	
7.	

© Network Educational Press

Pupils' contribution to school data

This chapter identifies at least four elements that can be identified in a pupil's learning behaviour:

- a breadth of activity and skills;

- an inquiring mind;

- a lively interest in and respect for other people;

- the pursuit of high achievement.

This list can be extended, particularly with personal skills and attributes. Adult and pupil learners have much to offer to the culture and climate of any school. Too often, only adults are invited to contribute thoughts about improving 'the way we do things around here'. Increasingly, schools see the need to hear from the pupils as well. You may well talk to your class already about how its members view school, feel about your lessons and what they enjoy doing. We know many of the behaviours which can arise when school is one factor which is unsatisfactory for them.

Asking the pupils

Kingsbrook Comprehensive School in Northamptonshire constructed a questionnaire to find out what pupil attitudes were in relation to their time spent in Year 11. The questionnaire was drawn up by a small group of senior staff and governors. Interestingly, it was the three governors who carried out the subsequent survey with the deputy head and collated the results. These were published in the staffroom. Bear this last point in mind when you see the subjects on which opinions were sought, and examples of summaries of the findings. As data, the results are extremely valuable for future teaching and learning.

Seventy students out of a Year 12 group of 150 were interviewed. The report comments: 'Obviously these were more representative of the more able as all those interviewed are currently in Year 12 following either GNVQ or 'A' level courses.'

The questionnaire included the following:

- Did you work hard for GCSE?

- What does working hard mean?

- Results - were these better/worse than expected - from your perspective?

- Were you worked hard?

- Did you have clear deadlines?

- Did you enjoy the subject?

- Was there equal treatment of boys and girls?

- Was the course clearly planned?

- Did others distract you?

- What teaching styles suited you best?

- Did you feel you received help and advice when needed?

- Overall, did you feel you got 'a good deal'?

- Any other comments?

The final eight-page report gave examples of a large number of individual comments. In the introduction, it is reported that 'The majority of students felt they had received "a good deal".' They were also reported as being very supportive of each other and very honest in their opinions.

Two examples of published information include:

What teaching styles suited you best?

Practical activity	43 responses
Discussion	36
Note taking	33
Active learning	26
Questions/answer	16
Essays	13
Teacher talking	11

(Student comments were added to the report of this question's responses)

Did others distract you?

9%	Subject A	21 responses
9%	Subject B	11
16%	Subject C	6
...		
...		
53%	Subject M	43
54%	Subject N	70

(Student comments were added)

The possibility of collecting data of this kind speaks well of climate and inter-personal confidence. *School Improvement: What can pupils tell us?*, edited by Jean Ruddock, Roland Chaplain and Gwen Wallace, provides a well researched and authoritative way into exploring what the client thinks. Importantly, the book refers closely to leading international research on school improvement and the need to search out the pupil view.

'Data is inert until someone handles it and makes it powerful'. School data is largely pupil data. Pupils should be contributing to, and feel empowered by, data which has the potential to improve their teaching and learning.

Action points

1. Write a list of pupil behaviours which you feel support effective teaching and learning. Attempt this task under two headings:
   - behaviour which improves subject attainment;
   - behaviour which supports personal development.

2. Read the OFSTED Handbook for schools, Section 4.

3. Identify three or four specific activities that all your class will experience in the coming 12 months, which support improved subject attainment and/or personal development.

4. Add the subject attainment targets for your class.

5. Identify three things you will seek to provide as class teacher, which support the fulfilment of points 3 and 4 above.

6. Identify two ways in which the school's resources, human and material, can support your ambitions for your class. Who can help you?

7. Find two ways in which parents might support their children's improvement this year. How will this be communicated to them? In school, who can help you?

8. What are your measurable success criteria for knowing whether you have been sufficiently successful in fulfilling your ambitions for your class? For example, 80% (or 95%, or even 100%) of pupils are ....

Making Pupil Data Powerful - a guide for classroom teachers

Sources of Further Information

This is not an exhaustive list. It is offered to you as a useful first reference, and relates mainly to materials used in the book.

Government agencies

*Asterisked titles distributed to, and available in, your school. Other publications usually available on request to:
DfEE Publications: Tel: 0845 602 2260
QCA Publications: Tel: 01787 884444

Setting targets to raise standards	DfEE	contains school case studies
From targets to action *	DfEE	contains examples of school practice
Autumn Package *	DfEE	also contains self/staff-development exercises
Standards at Key Stage 1/2/3/4 *	QCA	reporting annually to schools in Nov/Dec on national results at each key stage

Other sources of additional information

Books

The Numbers Game - Using Assessment Data in Primary Schools

The Numbers Game - Using Assessment Data in Secondary Schools

both by Keith Hedger and Professor David Jesson; available from Shropshire Education Publications, The Shirehall, Abbey Foregate, Shrewsbury SY2 6ND

Using Assessment Results for School Improvement by Mary James; Heinemann

Effective Learning Activities by Chris Dickinson; Network Educational Press

Effective Heads of Department by Phil Jones and Nick Sparks; Network Educational Press

School Improvement: What can pupils tell us? edited by Jean Ruddock, Roland Chaplain and Gwen Wallace; David Fulton

Support agencies

Centre for the Study of Comprehensive Schools (for broadsheets on *Using Assessment Results*), University of Leicester, Moulton College, Moulton, Northampton NN3 7RR

Curriculum, Evaluation and Management Centre (for information on ALIS, YELLIS, MIDYIS and PIPS), Burdon House, School of Education, University of Durham DH11TA

National Association for Primary Education (for broadsheets on *Using Assessment Results*), Queens Building, University of Leicester, Barrack Road, Northampton NN2 6AF

National Foundation for Educational Research (for information on Cognitive Ability Tests), The Mere, Upton Park, Slough SL1 2DQ

The Internet

You will find some of the government agency materials on these sites.
National Grid for Learning   http:/www.ngfl.gov.uk/
DfEE Standards Unit   http:www.standards.dfee.gov.uk/
QCA   http://www.qca.org.uk/
OFSTED   http://www.ofsted.gov.uk/ofsted.htm

Making Pupil Data Powerful - a guide for classroom teachers

THE SCHOOL EFFECTIVENESS SERIES

The School Effectiveness Series focuses on practical and useful ideas for individual schools and teachers. The series addresses the issues of whole school improvement along with new knowledge about teaching and learning, and offers straightforward solutions that teachers can use to make life more rewarding for themselves and those they teach.

Book 1: *Accelerated Learning in the Classroom* by Alistair Smith
ISBN: 1-85539-034-5   £15.95
- The first book in the UK to apply new knowledge about the brain to classroom practice
- Contains practical methods so teachers can apply accelerated learning theories to their own classrooms
- Aims to increase the pace of learning and deepen understanding
- Includes advice on how to create the ideal enviroment for learning and how to help learners fulfil their potential
- Offers practical solutions on improving performance, motivation and understanding

Book 2: *Effective Learning Activities* by Chris Dickinson
ISBN: 1-85539-035-3   £8.95
- An essential teaching guide which focuses on practical activities to improve learning
- Aims to improve results through effective learning, which will raise achievement, deepen understanding, promote self-esteem and improve motivation
- Includes activities which are designed to promote differentiation and understanding
- Includes activities suitable for GCSE, National Curriculum, Highers, GSVQ and GNVQ

Book 3: *Effective Heads of Department* by Phil Jones & Nick Sparks
ISBN: 1-85539-036-1   £8.95
- Contains a range of practical systems and approaches; each of the eight sections ends with a 'checklist for action'
- Designed to develop practice in line with OFSTED expectations and DfEE thinking by monitoring and improving quality
- Addresses issues such as managing resources, leadership, learning, departmental planning and making assessment valuable
- Includes useful information for senior managers in schools who are looking to enhance the effectiveness of their Heads of Department

Book 4: *Lessons are for Learning* by Mike Hughes
ISBN: 1-85539-038-8   £11.95
- Brings together the theory of learning with the realities of the classroom environment
- Encourages teachers to reflect on their own classroom practice and challenges them to think about why they teach in the way they do
- Offers practical suggestions for activities that bridge the gap between recent developments in the theory of learning and the constraints in classroom teaching
- Ideal for stimulating thought and generating discussion

Book 5: *Effective Learning in Science* by Paul Denley and Keith Bishop
ISBN: 1-85539-039-6   £11.95
- Encourages discussion about the aims and purposes in teaching science and the role of subject knowledge in effective teaching
- Tackles issues such as planning for effective learning, the use of resources and other relevant management issues
- Offers help in the development of a departmental plan to revise schemes of work, resources, classroom strategies, in order to make learning and teaching more effective
- Ideal for any science department aiming to increase performance and improve results

Book 6: *Raising Boys' Achievement* by Jon Pickering

ISBN: 1-85539-040-X   £11.95

- Addresses the causes of boys' underachievement and offers possible solutions
- Focuses the search for causes and solutions on teachers working in the classroom
- Looks at examples of good practice in schools to help guide the planning and implementation of strategies to raise achievement
- Offers practical, 'real' solutions, along with tried and tested training suggestions
- Ideal as a basis for INSET or as a guide to practical activities for classroom teachers

Book 7: *Effective Provision for Able & Talented Children* by Barry Teare

ISBN: 1-85539-041-8   £11.95

- Basic theory, necessary procedures and turning theory into practice
- Main methods of identifying the able and talented
- Concerns about achievement and appropriate strategies to raise achievement
- The role of the classroom teacher, monitoring and evaluation techniques
- Practical enrichment activities and appropriate resources

Book 8: *Effective Careers Education & Guidance* by Andrew Edwards and Anthony Barnes

ISBN: 1-85539-045-0   £11.95

- Strategic planning of the careers programme as part of the wider curriculum
- Practical consideration of managing careers education and guidance
- Practical activities for reflection and personal learning, and case studies where such activities have been used
- Aspects of guidance and counselling involved in helping students to understand their own capabilities and form career plans
- Strategies for reviewing and developing existing practice

Book 9: *Best behaviour and Best behaviour FIRST AID* by Peter Relf, Rod Hirst, Jan Richardson and GeorginaYoudell

ISBN: 1-85539-046-9   £12.95

- Provides support for those who seek starting points for effective behaviour management, for individual teachers and for middle and senior managers
- Focuses on practical and useful ideas for individual schools and teachers

Best behaviour FIRST AID

ISBN: 1-85539-047-7   £10.50 (pack of 5 booklets)

- Provides strategies to cope with aggression, defiance and disturbance
- Straightforward action points for self-esteem

Book 10: *The Effective School Governor* by David Marriott

ISBN 1-85539-042-6   £15.95 (including free audio tape)

- Straightforward guidance on how to fulfil a governor's role and responsibilities
- Develops your personal effectiveness as an individual governor
- Practical support on how to be an effective member of the governing team
- Audio tape for use in car or at home

Book 11: *Improving Personal Effectiveness for Managers* in Schools by James Johnson

ISBN 1-85539-049-3   £11.95

- An invaluable resource for new and experienced teachers in both primary and secondary schools
- Contains practical strategies for improving leadership and management skills
- Focuses on self-management skills, managing difficult situations, working under pressure, developing confidence, creating a team ethos and communicating effectively

Book 13: *Closing the Learning Gap* by Mike Hughes

    ISBN 1-85539-051-5   £15.95

- Helps teachers, departments and schools to close the Learning Gap between what we know about effective learning and what actually goes on in the classroom
- Encourages teachers to reflect on the ways in which they teach, and to identify and implement strategies for improving their practice
- Helps teachers to apply recent research findings about the brain and learning
- Full of practical advice and real, tested strategies for improvement
- Written by a teacher, for teachers, to stimulate thought and interest 'at a glance'

Other Publications

Accelerated Learning in Practice by Alistair Smith

    ISBN: 1-85539-048-5   £19.95

- The author's second book which takes Nobel Prize winning brain research into the classroom.
- Structured to help readers access and retain the information necessary to begin to accelerate their own learning and that of the students they teach.
- Contains over 100 learning tools, case studies from 36 schools and an up to the minute section.
- Includes 9 principles of learning based on brain research and the author's 7 Stage Accelerated Learning cycle.

Effective Resources for Able and Talented Children by Barry Teare

    ISBN: 1-85539-050-7   £24.95

- A practical sequel to Barry Teare's *Effective Provision for Able and Talented Children,* which can nevertheless be used entirely independently
- Contains a wealth of photocopiable resources for able and talented pupils in both the primary and secondary sectors
- Provides activities designed to inspire, motivate, challenge and stretch able children, encouraging them to enjoy their true potential
- Resources are organised into National Curriculum areas, such as Literacy, Science and Humanities, each preceded by a commentary outlining key principles and giving general guidance for teachers

Primary Publications

Imagine That... by Stephen Bowkett
    ISBN: 1-85539-043-4   £19.95
- Hands-on, user-friendly manual for stimulating creative thinking, talking and writing in the classroom
- Provides over 100 practical and immediately useable classroom activities and games that can be used in isolation, or in combination, to help meet the requirements and standards of the National Curriculum
- Explores the nature of creative thinking and how this can be effectively driven through an ethos of positive encouragement, mutual support and celebration of success and achievement
- Empowers children to learn how to learn

Helping With Reading by Anne Butterworth and Angela White
    ISBN: 1-85539-044-2   £14.95
- Includes sections on 'Hearing Children Read', 'Word Recognition' and 'Phonics'
- Provides precisely focused, easily implemented follow-up activities for pupils who need extra reinforcement of basic reading skills
- Activities which directly relate to the National Curriculum and 'Literacy Hour' group work. They are clear, practical and easily implemented. Ideas and activities can also be incorporated into Individual Education Plans
- Aims to address current concerns about reading standards and to provide support in view of the growing use of classroom assistants and parents to help with the teaching of reading

Please note that the prices given above are guaranteed until 1 January, 2000